C000092624

"Weerz me mam?"

A further collection of autobiographical
childhood stories of
the 40s and 50s
by Fred Pass

First Edition
© Copyright Jill E. Fitzpatrick

Printed and published by:
ALD Design & Print
279 Sharrow Vale Road
Sheffield S11 8ZF

Telephone 0114 267 9402

E-mail a.lofthouse@btinternet.com

ISBN 1-901587-66-5

First published September 2007

All rights reserved
No part of this publication may be reproduced, stored in a retrieval
system or transmitted in any form or by any means, electronic,
mechanical, photocopying, recording or otherwise, without the
written permission of the publisher and the copyright holder.

All views and comments printed in this book are those of the author
and should not be attributed to the publisher.

Cover photograph: My mother's family, the Stones, pictured in their yard
in Whitehouse Lane August 1942. I am pictured in my mother's arms
extreme left. Not in the picture are my mother's brothers Tom and Jim,
also my Aunty May who took the photograph.

This book is dedicated
to the memories of

Annette Chapman
and
Annie Marriott

Further Dedications to

Teachers:

Feinberg
Turner
Stone
Perry
Dowson
Whitham (Mrs)

and all ex pupils of Hillfoot school

Chapters Page

Foreword

I've lost count of people asking me the same question "When's your dad going to write another book to follow his successful "Weerz me Dad"?"

My dad got fed up with me pestering him so much that he handed me loads of his work, much of it written years ago, and said "Get on with it." I'm obviously biased, but I think that he has a talent that should not be wasted.

If you liked "Weerz me Dad?" then this is a must have book, full of nostalgia and laughter, a true reminder of life in the forties and fifties.

Every word in this book is my dad's, I take no credit for its content. Along with the help of Roger Marsh we have put together a book full of laughs, anxieties, and sometimes sadness.

The only stipulation made by my dad was that St. Luke's Hospice should benefit in someway or other.

My dad won't thank me for mentioning it but all his previous writing has earned over £35,000 for his favourite charity St. Luke's Hospice.

Enjoy the book.

Jill E. Fitzpatrick

Me Mam and Dad

Introduction

For "Weerz me Mam?" we return to the 1940s of Martin Street, Sheffield. It is a return to the hardships of post war Sheffield and its working class living conditions, in our case a back-to-back, one-up-one down house.

The 1940s in Sheffield was, as in all English working class areas, a time of shortages. Food was still rationed, home entertainment consisted of a wireless (radio), and Social Services were practically non-existent. People survived in many cases, not in spite of each other, but because of each other.

Reflecting on those times produced heroes for me, not least Mrs. Aistrop who lived facing us in our yard on

3

Martin Street. Mr. and Mrs. Aistrop brought up eight children in the most basic of conditions.

She would often come into our house, her conversations would begin with "Hasta (have you) got this?" or "Hasta got that?" So much so that my dad had nicknamed her 'Lady Aster' (a rich socialite of the times). If he saw Mrs. Aistrop heading for our house he would often say "Shiz 'ear Lady Aster."

Her request to borrow something would cover a multitude of things, anything in fact. It could be a couple of eggs, or a shovel full of coal, and one request was "Can a borra ya fryin pan forran hour?" She was, nevertheless, always welcome. For whatever Mrs. Aistrop's shortages might have been, these could have been ours at anytime. In other words we were all in the same boat. Mrs. Aistrop borrowing was on behalf of the kids, never ever for herself. Looking back she must have had the constitution of a carthorse to survive the many hardships that the times threw up.

Remarkably Mrs. Aistrop lived to be 92. I was privileged to attend her funeral in April 2007. She had lost her eldest, Audrey, through cancer a few years previously. All the other seven were at her funeral to pay homage, with all seven looking well, a fitting tribute to a tenacious working class woman. I was just thankful that I was able to attend.

The characters in the first half of this book are almost the same as in "Weerz me Dad?" Dennis Aistrop, Mrs. Aistrop's oldest son, and Pete Marshall another lad who lived in our yard, Peter tragically died at a young age, as mentioned in "Weerz me Dad?"

Lawrence Jenkinson, another close neighbour, was a ginger haired lad with constant wobbly eyes. Another amazing fact emerges, Lawrence went on to own three or four shops. What kind of shops? Opticians what else!

The first half of the book is of my earliest memories in the middle forties to when we moved in 1952 to Boyland Place, Neepsend. It is also of my schooldays at Woodside School, Rutland Road, Burngreave School and finally to Hillfoot School; and my workplace John Bedfords as a trainee machine fitter.

I hope you enjoy the journey.

Fred Pass

Chapter 1

"Weerz me Mam?"

My mother Gladys died in 1997 just a couple of months short of her 84th birthday. Towards the back end of her life she was housebound and almost blind due to cataract problems. She had endured, like thousands of others, a hard working class life. Despite always being short of money she had never worked, due to the fact that my dad thought it was his place to work, and my mothers place to look after everything else.

She was a barrier for every day problems for my dad hence her regular saying, "Don't tell ya dad." If I was ever going to do something that she did not approve of she would say in a stern voice, "Ah should think so," other than that she would say nothing but would stay silent in her disapproval.

So, "Weerz me Mam?" is in fact a contradiction. For we always knew where she was, in the house. Whatever, she would be there for us.

If you ever told her a story that would surprise her she would sometimes exclaim, "Goods Gollies."

Any sort of problems she would be there to sort them out. She managed the house keeping during hard times on the principle if we had not got the money for anything, we would do without. Her one vice was having a bet on the horses and later in life, the bingo.

She seemed to me to get better the older she was despite her health problems. She sort of mellowed. If she did not approve of something she could be annoying by just sitting there in silence.

Up to her death, she still dealt in 'Old Money'. One day late in her life she asked me to get her some prawns. When I did so and told her they cost 60p she replied, "Twelve bob for prawns, I'm not having any more of them."

She was mainly looked after in her final years by my older brother Brian, also the Social Services people were of great help. The only complaint she would have was as she would say, "I've got money nah and av nowt to spend it on. When ah think back on all the hardship me and ya dad had to put up with it makes ya want to cry."

She could find something good in anything; she could eat a slice of bread and butter and say something like, "That butter was nice."

I once remarked about an article in the newspaper where a young bloke had beaten up an old age pensioner and took her money. She made comments of, "That poor old lady...," and amazing to me, "...and that poor young bloke. What is society like when some youngster has to revert to that?"

She was so trusting; every time I visited her the back door would be open. I was always telling her to keep the back door locked to which she would answer, "If I've got to lock myself in the house its time to pack up."

On visiting her one-day she told me that two teenage girls used to visit her, and they were very kind volunteering for a number of things. She said they turned up every Saturday at two o'clock. So having my suspicions without telling my mother I made sure that I was there the following week.

At two o'clock the two women turned up. My worries were unfounded for they turned out to be Jehovah's Witnesses. So don't believe all the bad comments made about that religion. These two young women were really doing good. The particular day in question made me laugh. One of the young women said, "Hello Mrs. Pass, can we do some shopping for you?" to which my mother replied, "Oh no love our Brian's done me shoppin." Then the girl went on, "Can we make you a cup of tea then?" "No," my mother said, "Our Fred 'ere has just made me one." "Well," said the girl "is there anything we can do for you?" Her answer left me laughing, "Are you gooin' anywhere near a betting shop?"

Saturday night was probably the only night when my mother used to go to the pub with my dad. I would be in the house with my brother Brian. Sometimes, unbeknown to our parents, we would go down to the Burlington Pub pull ourselves up by the railings on the half frosted windows and have a peek inside. There would be a bloke on a piano and everyone would have a singsong. We would know when it was closing time because the last song would be, "It's a long way to Tipperary." A thought that has always stuck in my mind was what do they sing in Tipperary on a boozy Saturday night? So once they started to sing this song Brian and I would leg it back home so no one would be the wiser.

On going out we would never lock the door. We would never be afraid of burglars in those days, not because of people's honesty but due to the fact that we had nowt worth pinching.

As a young kid I waited with some trepidation because there would always be an argument of sorts, probably the only time my mother and dad had a proper argument. It would always be about my dad's mother. We had a framed picture of her over the fireplace. My dad idolised his mother, so when he'd had a few pints he would wax lyrical about his mother's qualities. He would stare at the photo and say something like, "The best mother in the world," and my mother would mumble, "She'd frighten you to death." By all accounts she was a bit of a firebrand. Her mumbled comments would at first be ignored by my dad, but not for long.

He would then start to reminisce. He would bring me into the equation by saying, "Does tha see her Fred lad? Ya kno when I left school the teacher presented me with the punishment book because I'd been named in it the most times. Well I took the book home and when mi mam saw it she went mad. She said, "According to this book you've had cane twenty eight times last year. Is that true?" I said, "Yes," and mi mam replied, "Come on we're going straight back to school." "She marched into the classroom and confronted the teacher in question asking, "Have you caned my lad twenty eight times?" the teacher answered in the affirmative so she grabbed his cane and started hitting the teacher on his back as hard as she could. She counted every stroke out loud, "One, two, three..." etc., until she reached twenty eight, and then she announced, "...and one for good luck" whack."

On many a Saturday night my dad would regularly recall this story. My mother would chip in saying, "She'd have been better telling you to behave yourself," to which dad would react by saying she was looking after her kids. He would then go on about when he was a kid he and his brothers and sisters would run around with no shoes on. My mother's comeback to such stories was short, but as sharp as a needle, "That's nowt clever. We never ran around with no shoes on."

Eventually this sparring would lead to a full-blown argument and I along with my brother would be sent to bed. On one particular Saturday I anticipated the usual argument and in an effort to quell any trouble I turned the picture of my grandma, round, to face the wall. This only aggravated the situation and made it worse.

On entering our house my dad immediately accused my mother of turning the picture round resulting in an even more antagonistic argument. These rows used to worry me as a little kid.

On the Sunday morning after the Saturday night hullabaloo, I would dash down stairs. If my mother wasn't in I'd say to my dad, "Weerz me mam, dad?" and repeat, "Weerz me mam?" so quickly that it was sometimes lost in translation. My dad would ask, "What ya sayin?" and I'd repeat, "Weerz me mam?" to which my dad would counter with a laugh, "She's run away with a blackman." When all along she'd be gossiping on some neighbour's doorstep. On her re-entering our house I would breathe a sigh of relief.

They got on really well; any sort of confrontation by my mother to my dad would be by acidic quips.

My dad had an allotment up Rivelin that never seemed to produce much. Whenever my Uncle Ern called, the topic of conversation a lot of times was my dad's allotment. My mother would inject little acid remarks to which my dad would do his best to ignore; as an example:

Uncle Ernest: "How's allotment goin Fred?"

Dad: "Not so bad, I'm hoping for a good harvest this year."

Uncle Ern: "How wast last year?"

Dad: "Not too good."

My mothers quip: "Three tomatoes."

Dad: "Ave used plenty of manure on me tomatoes this year."

Mam's quip: "God knows what they'll taste like."

Uncle Ern: "Will it have been worthwhile having allotment Fred?"

Dad: "Oh argh."

Mam's quip: "It's been a success alreight. Six months for three tomatoes."

Dad still ignoring mam: "Am hopin fo sum nice spuds this year."

Mam's quip: "Two spuds to go we three tomatoes, It wouldn't feed a chuffin church mouse."

My dad would start to crack: "Ya said three

tomatoes. I remember like yesterday you with a fryin pan full of tomatoes."

Mam: "Aye only cuz Mr. Hill next door gave us some of his. Waste a time that allotment, about 500-times backurds and forurds to Rivelin. What for? I'll tell thi somat. I'm not fryin tomatoes that's been covered by horse muck. It'll stink house arght."

Dad: "Ah thought tha wo ironin, keep thi noorse arght an ger-ron wi what that doin."

Me mam: "Listnin to thee's a better laugh, than listnin tut wireless (sarcastically) looking forrad to a good harvest. Ave never heard out as daft in me life."

As a row would be about to erupt Ernest would say "Am off Fred lad, see ya later." I'd soon follow, to call for one of my mates to keep out of the firing line.

Years later nothing had changed. My wife and I called at my parent's house when they were living on the Arbourthorne Estate. My dad was sitting his head forward hands on his knees staring at the television. My mother was sitting reading a newspaper. My dad welcomed us by saying, "Nah then Fred, have a pike at this lot," (translated means have a look at this). On the television was a live broadcast of a non manned rocket launch from Cape Canaveral, America. "Chuffin marvellous init, thi granddad drove a horse'n cart, now thi sending rockets into space." We both sat down joining my dad to watch this space shot. They

13

started the count down, only to announce they had problems and the space shot was aborted. They added they were looking into what had caused the postponement.

My mother lowered her paper and said, "It'll be a faulty connection."
Dad: "Tha what, what tha gooin on abarht?"
Mother: "It'll be somthin not catchin."
Dad: "Not chuffin catchin. Don't talk so chuffin daft."
Mother: "It's obvious. One at thingys, it'll not be catchin."
Dad: "One at thingys. Tha sees all them blokes sat in front of all them computers, does tha kno what they are?" Without waiting for an answer he went on, "...well al tell thi shalah thi only rocket scientists that's all, between um thi'll ave abaght a million qualifications and thart ere six thousand miles away, and thar knows strait away."
Mother: "Well it's obvious."
Dad: (Mockingly a hand cupped to one side of his mouth, shouting at the telly) "Don't bother lads. Our owd lass'l tell ya problem. It's a faulty thingy, it's causin a faulty connection." He went on, "...av heard chuffin lot nah. Ah don't know why thi bother wi them encyclopaedia whats its". My dad looked at me, "Az tha ever heard owt like it."

I answered in total silence. I changed the subject, being careful not to bring the allotment into the conversation. My mother disappeared behind her paper. After about twenty minutes or so there was an announcement from America that the space shot had been abandoned due to a faulty connection. My dad was struck dumb by this announcement. My mother lowered the newspaper and said, "I'll put kettle on. We'll have a cuppa tea."

Visiting my mother in her later years, I was always trying to get her to reminisce but it was hard work, in fact like getting blood out of a stone. The conversation would go something like:

Me: "Mam where did ya meet mi dad?"

Mam: "Oh ah don't kno."

Me: "Howduya mean ya don't kno?"

Mam: "Cus ah don't."

Me: "Ya were married for forty odd years an ya can't remember?"

Mam: "It worra long time ago."

Me: "Did ya meet in a pub?"

Mam: "No, we'd not got money for beer."

Me: "What did ya think when you first saw him?"

Mam: "What a daft question to ask."

Me: "Was he well built when he were a young bloke?"

Mam: "Not really."

Me: "So what kind of build was he then?"

Mam: "He was a bit ont wiry side."

Me: "What kind of build is wiry?"

Mam: "Just a bit wiry that's all."

Me: "Where did ya get married then?"

Mam: "St. Phillips Church."

Me: "Ave never seen your wedding photo's."

Mam: "That's cuz thi weren't none."

Me: "Chuffin ell it couldn't have been much of a wedding then."

Mam. "It weernt. An ya can stop asking me questions, ya making me dizzy."

Chapter 2

There ain't no justice

It was the start of a new term at Crookesmoor and I got a tremendous boost because Dennis Aistrop, who was a year younger than me, was promoted to our class. He was so far advanced academically it was decided he would benefit being in an older class.

At the start of a new term, our teacher would set a test exam, to set up a sort of league table of forty five pupils. The first test was maths; I was excited at this for Dennis. I thought just wait till they see how good my pal is. After marking the efforts of the class the teacher would read out the results starting at the bottom. Number forty five then upwards. He would start ridiculing the bottom lad; his comments would get milder as he went up the league table, but nevertheless, no encouragement.

By the time he got to me I'd finished in sixth place, which I thought, was quite good. "Pass," he addressed me. "Your effort was poor, you should have done better." The statement could, or should have done better roughly translated means, "I'm a good teacher and he's a bad pupil." That's why it's the most frequent phrase used by teachers. He went on. His closing comment pleased me, it shouldn't have but it did. "I'm beginning to lose all interest in you," he concluded. I thought, "I've lost all interest in you ages ago."

Up to now there had been no mention of Dennis. I couldn't wait for him to get to number one. As he announced, "Number one, Aistrop," my heart skipped a beat. Good old Dennis I was thinking, as he called Dennis to the front of the class. What's the teacher going to do I thought, perhaps ask us all to give him a round of applause, or three cheers, it must be something like that, its got to be some sort of adulation.

The teacher looked at Dennis disdainfully, and then ordered Dennis to stand on a chair facing the class. The teacher then picked up his cane, and began pointing his cane at items of Dennis' clothing. "Look at this," he said pointing at a hole in Dennis' jumper, "And what about these," he added pointing at the holes in Dennis' shoes. I cringed at Dennis' humiliation; "Turn round," the teacher ordered, and pointing to the holes in Dennis' trousers arse said, "Can't your parents do better than this?" Dennis was blood red with embarrassment. The teacher then demanded Dennis to hold out his hands. "Filthy," the teacher declared. He then said, "Go to the toilets and wash them and be quick about it."

Dennis dashed off; during his absence the whole class sat in complete silence.

We could all hear the tap running in the distance, and then Dennis' footsteps on his way back to class.

When Dennis returned, the teacher inspected Dennis' hands and said, "That's better," then ordered Dennis to hold out his hand brought the cane down on it causing Dennis to winch. The teacher then said, "Go back to your seat Aistrop and don't ever come in my class with dirty hands again."

The teacher in question was tall and thin. He had a huge hooked nose and wore thick glasses, without them he was almost blind. He was knocked kneed and if his feet were fingers on a clock his left foot would have been pointing to ten while his right foot would be pointing at two. He was a humourless bombastic sort of bloke whose appearance mirrored his personality.

Playtimes at school in the fifties were mainly spent playing football in the schoolyard; the game was a bit manic to say the least. It was played with about fifty a side. One novelty factor at the time was the fact that we had a German lad at Crookesmoor. His name was Klaus.

During one of the impromptu football games Klaus volleyed this big rubber ball at my thighs, causing a great stinging pain. What hurt me more was the fact that he started laughing at my obvious pain. I pushed Klaus in retaliation, he pushed back and the next minute we were rolling about, in a sort of wrestle on the floor. All the kids were gathered round chanting "A FEIGHT." "A FEIGHT." "A FEIGHT."

The next thing was this teacher, on playground duty separates us and orders us into a nearby classroom, "What are you fighting for?" he demanded. I went on about Klaus kicking the ball at me and causing me pain, then laughing about it. The teacher then looked at Klaus and said "Well?" Klaus who could virtually speak no English jabbered on at the teacher in German. The teacher looked on in bewilderment, obviously not understanding a word. He scratched his chin then bellowed out to Klaus in a Tarzan sort of English, pointing and saying, "You go."

To me he said, "This school will not tolerate such behaviour," and gave me two strokes of the cane before adding, "Behave yourself in future." I felt aggrieved; the teacher had acted as judge and jury, punishing me on the evidence against me given in a language he didn't understand.

At assembly one morning the head teacher announced to the school that some woodwork tools had gone missing. These were from one of the prefab type classrooms that were situated on one side of the tip facing the school. He went on to say that serious enquiries would take place and the culprit would be found.

Boys and girls were separated, so it was a surprise to see the head teacher march into the class with Margaret Marshall, little Pete's older sister. He ordered her to stand on a chair. Then pointing to her said to the class, "You are now looking at a thief." Margaret had already been caned for the offence, but had to endure this humiliation in every classroom of the school. The only evidence was that she had been seen that evening playing near the prefab that housed the missing woodwork items.

A couple of weeks later a lad was caught for the offence, he was trying to sell the tools and was caught by the police. Did Margaret receive an apology to put the record straight? Not a chance.

Chapter 3

It's turned out cold again

Living in a back-to-back, one up one down house in 1950 meant freezing dark winter mornings. I'd get up for school to find my mother struggling to get a fire started using rolled up paper, sometimes she'd have a few sticks if she was lucky.

On such mornings breakfast would be a slice of bread and dripping. My dad worked three shifts - mornings 6am till 2pm, afternoons 2pm till 10pm, and nights 10pm till 6am. When my dad was on nights we'd get up to a roaring fire, which was most welcome. But that was only one week out of three. On such weeks breakfast was tea and toast as my mother was good at baking. The bread would be uncut so the toast would be about three quarters of an inch thick, covered in butter and a lot more welcome than bread and dripping.

In the winter of 1950 Dennis had a brainwave. He suggested we could chop a bundle of sticks of wood and sell them at two pence a bundle. He figured all we needed was wood, transport of any kind and a hatchet. He reasoned we could get the wood from White's fruit shop. Mr White was always sympathetic to young kids. Dennis said he'd got the transport in the shape of an old pram. The pram in question was a high slung affair, a real posh looking vehicle that looked out of place on Martin Street.

The pram had known better days, it was covered in muck and all the upholstery was ripped. It was parked permanently in the corner of our yard. Whenever we went to the coke house Dennis used to have to use this pram to fetch the cokes in. It always caused him great embarrassment as all the other kids would call out "Lord Aistrop" and similar micky taking names.

Straight away I said "I'm not pushing that." Dennis said he'd got someone in mind. He called over to little Pete Marshall with the words "Do ya want to come wiv us to make some money?" Little Pete with short trousers that settled just below the knee, and wearing hob nailed boots, and stockings that were invariably one up one down, was all for it. "What do I have to do?" said Pete. "Push that," Dennis replied pointing to the pram. "O.K." Pete quickly responded.

Dennis said the only problem was that we hadn't got a hatchet. "We've got one" I retorted. Dennis reasoned that we would have to sell our sticks away from Martin Street for he said our mothers would claim any money we made, so we agreed to keep it a secret from our parents.

I dashed into our house for the hatchet. It must have been Monday because my mother was doing the weekly wash in a big washtub. I hated washday because the house was always full of steam. "What ya up to?" my mother snapped. "Nowt," I replied disappearing down the cellar. As I emerged clutching the hatchet my mother said, "An where do ya think ya goin with that mi lad?" Not able to reveal the real reason I replied "Wi playin at cowboys and Indians," "Oh no ya not," responded my mother, "Yull cause somebody real damage wi that." "Ah but mam," I started to reply, "Neer mind ah but, ya not taking that hatchet out of this house."

Mournfully I walked back outside to Dennis and Pete to tell them about our misfortune. Dennis said "Will ya mam be going to the shops?" "No," I said, "Shiz doin't weshin." Dennis said we'd have to find a way to get my mother away from the house for five minutes, and then I could sneak in and dash off with the hatchet. After we had completed our stick selling venture I could drop our hatchet down our cellar grate and my mother would be no wiser.

"Go and sit in your house," said Dennis, "Ill think of summat." I forlornly walked back in and sat by the door. My mother gave me a suspicious look and queried "What ya moping at?" "Nowt," I replied. "Ah kno you milad. Ya up to no good and I've had your messing up to here," she countered holding the back of her hand under her chin. I sat looking at the floor.

Moments later there was a knock on the door, Dennis popped his head round the door and said "Mrs. Pass, Mrs. Theaker wants ya." "What's she want?" asked my mother. Dennis came back with, "Ah don't know." My mother walked out of the door and up our entry to go to Mrs. Theaker's who lived in the next yard.

As she went out of sight Dennis said, "Quick." I got the hatchet from the cellar head and Dennis, pram pushing

Pete, and myself with our hatchet were off down Martin Street to White's fruit shop.

"What ya after lads?" Mr. White greeted the three of us. "Have you any boxes?" said Dennis. Mr. White looked around quickly and found four plywood type boxes that had been containers for lettuce. "Only these lads," said Mr. White adding, "Are they any good tu ya?" "Well have em," said Dennis, "but those banana boxes would be better." Banana boxes were coffin shaped and made from proper wood. "Oh ya can't have them," said Mr. White, "There's a five bob deposit on them."

We came away with the plywood boxes and were feeling down in the mouth. We walked down Burlington Street with long faces. Dennis perked up suddenly when he'd noticed The Burlington pub's back yard door ajar. "Come on," he said. We peeked into the back yard and low and behold the yard was stacked up with empty wooden beer crates. Quick as a flash we nicked half a dozen beer crates and we were off to the top of Martin Street loaded up with boxes.

We turned a blind eye to the words on the side of the beer crates, 'Returnable two and sixpence'. The lettuce boxes and beer crates were held together with steel banding which we used to hold the bundles of sticks together. Dennis and I took it in turns to do the chopping and due to the steel bands it proved hard work and we soon had sore hands.

Anyway after what seemed like forever we had the pram loaded up with bundles of sticks. Dennis reasoned the price would be two pence, because he said you could buy sticks from the shop for three pence, therefore ours would be a bargain, and delivered to the door. Dennis also suggested we sell our wares away from Martin Street, keeping our stick selling business a secret from our parents. We all agreed on trying Oxford Street.

The first couple of houses just responded with a curt, "No." The third house took us aback. I knocked on the door and Dennis holding out a bunch of sticks in each hand said "Do you want some firewood?" to which the bloke whose house it was said, "Thanks," took the sticks and slammed the door in our faces.

We were downcast at the early response, but decided to carry on. We were uplifted by our next port of call. We knocked on the door. A dog immediately began to bark, which unnerved me being scared of dogs. The woman of the house opened the door and the dog came out barking around our ankles. Dennis was quickly into his sales pitch. "Do ya want to buy some sticks?" quickly adding due, to the earlier response, "Tuppence a bundle." The woman seemed genuinely pleased replying, "Oh I'll have three bundles," and adding "Just let me get my purse."

As she was disappearing back into the house the dog was still barking at us. With her back to us she called out, "If the dogs bothering you just kick its balls." Quick as a flash Pete duly obliged, with a swift kick with his hob nailed boots, and the dog shot off out of sight yelping. We all looked at each other in shock horror when the woman added, "You'll find them behind the bin."

All three of us peered behind the bin to see two tennis balls. We were looking at each other wide eyed, and lips stretched as the woman reappeared with her purse. She handed over sixpence enquiring, "Where's the dog?" not waiting for a reply she shut the door saying, "That dogs gets dafter."

Our sprits were lifted at our first sale. Then disaster, who should we bump into but Pete's mother Mrs. Marshall and his sister Margaret. "What you up to?" asked Mrs. Marshall. "We've been getting some sticks for you mam," replied Pete. "Oh you are good lads," said Mrs. Marshall, "Come on your mams will be proud of ya." Dennis and I managed to squeeze out a smile, and at the same time looking daggers at Pete.

As we entered our yard my mother was hanging out the washing. Mrs. Marshall called out to my mother, "Ere Gladys, just look what thiv been up to," pointing at the bundles of sticks. My mother looked at the bundles of sticks and said, "That's why ya wanted hatchet and that's why ah were sent on a wild goose chase to Theaker's". As Pete's mother, Dennis' mother, and my mother divided the sticks between them my mother asked me, "Why didn't you tell me that's what you wanted hatchet for?" I replied with a deadpan expression, "I just wanted to surprise ya mam."

The winter of 1950 brought, as winters do, snow. Dennis whose mind never rested said, "I've had an idea." Without letting him explain I said, "No chance," the stick selling venture was still fresh in my mind. Dennis insisted I listen saying, "All we need is a brush, a shovel and a box of salt." Dennis went on, he'd got a shovel, all I had to do would be to get a brush which wouldn't be hard as there was always an upturned brush out side our door. Women in those days could be regularly seen sweeping up outside their houses.

Pete was listening and quickly volunteered to get the salt. His request was turned down due to the fact we held him responsible for us losing our bundles of sticks. Lawrence Jenkinson was up for it. Lawrence's parents were out working all day and he was left in the charge of his grandmother who lived next door. Too honest for his own good Lawrence asked his grandmother for some salt. When she found out what he wanted it for, his request was quickly turned down, she said, "It would be like chuckin money int street." So we were left with only one possible helper, little Pete. We told him we would give him one last chance. Pete keen as ever was soon in and out of their house, coming out with a box of salt up his jumper.

Dennis as always applied logic; it was no good clearing snow from the houses on Martin Street, because no one would pay you for doing a job they could do themselves. Dennis said Crookesmoor Road would be a good place. Right at the very top of Crookesmoor Road, there was Barber Road, across Barber Road, Crookesmoor Road continued, "Big Victorian semis would be perfect," said Dennis. "Posh people lived there, they're sort of folks who live ont hill," he said.

So armed with brush, shovel and salt we were off.

Dennis said, "We would not ask people if they wanted the snow clearing service, we would complete the task, and then more or less we would have to be paid."

Dennis had a hole in his trousers arse; sometimes the flap of his shirt would stick out of the hole. Coming from a big family in hard times meant his footwear was poor, Dennis' toes use to stick out of his shoes, sometimes he would pull his socks down to cover his toes, which after a while resulted in holes in his socks, as we set of I noticed Dennis' socks had become ankle length, and not knee length due to him repositioning his socks to accommodate the holes in his shoes. Pete had got his regulation hob nailed boots. I was wearing a pair of old Wellingtons that at one time belonged to my brother Brian. I hated wearing them but Wellingtons represented winter footwear, summer footwear was slippers. I hated Wellingtons because they would leave a round sore ring around my calves.

When I first wore them they fitted all right, but now they were so small they popped as I took them off. My mother said Wellingtons were, to use her words, "Serviceable", which translated meant they would last forever.

Anyway we were soon at the top of Crookesmoor Road. It was freezing cold but Dennis reasoned we'd soon warm up doing our path clearing. Dennis spotted a posh looking house and we swung into action, Dennis shovelling, me sweeping and Pete scattering his salt. An old lady opened the door, "Wiv cleaned ya path missis," I said. She looked down at us in horror and said, "Well you've been trespassing," going on "You had no right to, get away from my door you scruffy little sods or I'll call the police." In 1950 there was no racial discrimination, that would come much later, but her attitude showed there was plenty of social discrimination about. In other words she didn't like us just by looking at us.

We carried on with our snow clearing efforts, getting between two pence and three pence each for our efforts. The wind was getting up and flakes of snow were blowing in our faces. We had about a bob apiece and each of us numb with the weather. Dennis said we would do one more then we'd call it a day.

Soaked and frozen we completed the last house. Dennis knocked on the door, as with the first house an old lady answered, "Wiv cleaned your path missus," Dennis declared. She looked at her path and said "Oh you have done a good job boys," despite the fact the path was quickly turning back into being covered by the snow which was falling heavily now. "Oh," she went on, "You look frozen stiff," adding, "Please come in and have a warm." The old lady led us into her front room. It was like stepping into a warm welcoming bath. "Sit yourselves down boys," we sat on a big settee facing the fire. She put a fireguard on one side and told us to put our socks on it to dry out. We did so, she then said, "I'll go and get you a warm drink."

As we waited we stared around the room in wonder. She had as an ornament a stuffed squirrel in a glass case on the sideboard. All the room was covered in carpet. On the mantle piece there was an oval shaped clock, in the silence the clock sent out a noise that sounded sort of posh. It didn't tick but slowly tocked, it was tock, and after what seemed long intervals tock. Our clock at home was a tin type of effort which seemed to be racing itself tick, tock, tick, tock, I looked round in wonderment, thinking, "Chuffin ell even clocks posh."

As the old lady returned we were sniffing away due to the warm room. She entered by carrying a tray with three cups and saucers on it plus a plate with half a dozen chocolate biscuits. She placed the tray on the floor saying, "Help yourselves boys." She looked down on us in a warm sympathetic sort of manner, as though she was looking down on a bucket full of kittens. She then left the room saying "Aren't I silly? I've not done myself a cup of tea." She returned with her cup of tea declaring "Oh I seem to have forgotten to put some chocolate biscuits on the plate." She had but they had been devoured the moment she left the room.

She sat in a chair opposite, and asked us all our names what our dads did for a living, where we lived and all sorts of friendly questions. In between the questions she praised us at regular intervals saying, "Oh you are good lads," and, "Working hard in such bad weather," all sorts of praise. She said, "And what are you going to do with the money you earn, give it to your mothers?" We all nodded in agreement but each one of us thinking, "Not chuffin likely."

She disappeared again asking, "Whose shoes and socks are these?" She was referring to Dennis' footwear.

When she reappeared she had a pair of old boy's shoes and socks, not new but a thousand times better than he already had. Dennis tried them on and looked as pleased as punch. The old lady said to Dennis, "Do you want me to throw these away?" referring to Dennis' previous footwear. "No," said Dennis I'll hang on to them (nothing got thrown away in the Aistrop house).

We must have been in the house the best part of an hour, when the woman said, "Right boys how much do I owe you?" We just sort of hunched our shoulders, probably overcome by the woman's kindness. "Will half a crown do?" she asked. I nodded in response trying to work out how to divide half a crown between three of us. To our amazement and delight, she proceeded to give us half a crown each. She waved us goodbye at her door saying, "Anytime boys you are welcome to clean my path." By the time we were leaving the path we had cleaned was congested again by snow. Dennis whispered out of the corner of his mouth, "We'll be back tomorra."

We felt on top of the world walking down Crookesmoor Road each clutching our half a crowns, plus the jangle of the change each of us had in our pockets. What a day I was thinking. We noticed ahead of us the old lady that had accused us of trespassing talking to a policeman, and pointing in our direction. "Nowt to worry about," said Dennis, "She gora path dun fo nowt."

As we passed the policeman gave me a great slap on the back of the head with his leather gloved covered hand. His slap sent me sprawling in the snow. He then picked me up with the scruff of the neck asking, "Where do ya come from?" When the lights came back on I stuttered "Martin Street." "Well get back to where you belong, if I see you again up here I'll have ya locked up."

All three of us dashed in the direction of Martin Street. Then to my horror I realised that due to being knocked over I'd lost my half a crown. When we got to Barber Road I told Dennis and Pete of my misfortune we all looked round. The policeman was still there and Crookesmoor Road where my half a crown was covered in an inch of snow. So if you happen to have found half a crown in Barber Road in 1950 it's mine. Due to my mishap did the other two share their money with me? Not chuffin likely.

At the first sight of rain in Martin Street, we'd scamper to the cobblers on the corner of Martin Lane. The cobbler was a small bloke with a huge hump on his back. We nicknamed him 'Umpy', the nickname was not meant to be cruel in any way, and it was just an obvious descriptive word. So if it ever started raining it would be, "Come on lets go to 'Umpy's."

'Umpy' was a really nice bloke to kids and would always make us welcome. We would peer over the counter and watch 'Umpy' hard at work. He would greet us with, "Yuv just come right lads av got kettle on." He would give us a huge pint pot of tea, out of which each of us would have a drink, and then pass it on. He would talk of football matches he had seen, his stories went down well with us, for 'Umpy' was a 'Wednesdayite'. He would sometimes give us a boiled sweet apiece. I always remember him as a really good bloke.

Many's the time I would be coming home from the first house at the Oxford Cinema at about 8 o'clock, and see 'Umpy's' shop still lit up by a single bulb. 'Umpy' still hard at work, sat amongst piles of old shoes, and all sorts of leather work. As a little kid I always felt sorry for 'Umpy'. I thought that being sat doubled up, hour after hour was the reason for him having a hump on his back. To us kids his shop and his manner were like a bright oasis in a desert of gloom.

To fill in the hours of a winters evening we would go round knocking on doors and ask, "Ave ya gor any owd papers ya don't want?" When we gathered an armful apiece we would then go to the chip shop on Martin Street plonk the newspapers on the counter and be rewarded by a big bag of chips each. We would always request, "Can ya put a lot of scrapings on?" Scrapings were little balls of fat that when added to the chips and covered in salt and vinegar tasted smashing. Plus the bonus of a small bag of chips transformed into a big bag of chips.

Collecting newspapers and then trading them in for a bag of chips was a good way of passing the time, and at the end of it you had something to show for your efforts. As in all good things there would be some fly in the ointment. In this case it was in the shape of a woman who worked part time at the chip shop. Her name was Phyllis, whenever she was serving, we would only get one bag of chips between us. She would always turn down our requests for scrapings. So in effect she made our paper collecting a waste of time. The way she looked at us, told us she could not stand the sight of us.

One particular night four of us did our paper collecting round, little Pete, Dennis, Lawrence and myself. As we approached the chip shop we sent Pete ahead to see who was in the chip shop. Pete dashed off in front such was our dislike for Phyllis, Dennis concocted a nickname for her, she was a slim woman with no visible chin, she became known as 'Filleted Phyllis'. On getting ahead of us Pete swung round and shouted to us "Don't bother its 'Filleted Phyllis'. "All that chuffin collecting fo nowt," I declared. "What a waste o time," added Lawrence.

Dennis being the brains of the outfit suggested that we each save our papers and go the next night, with any luck 'Filleted Phyllis' would not be working.

The next night we got the all clear from Pete, 'Filleted Phyllis' was absent. We all got a bag of chips, including scrapings. After eating our chips we were each left with a bundle of greasy chip paper, Dennis remarked that if only we had a match, he could find good use for the bundles of greasy paper. Quick as a flash Lawrence produced a box of matches. Lawrence came from a household that was slightly better off than the rest of us. A box of matches going missing in our house would be noticed straight away. Not in the Jenkinson household however, Lawrence even had piano lessons. Despite all this Jenks was still one of us. Dennis declared, "Good un Jenks lets go pay 'Filleted Phyllis' a call." She lived on the next road to the chip shop, so off we went.

As we went on our way Dennis reminded us of his dad's party trick one bonfire night, when all the kids had quickly used up their fireworks. He put on an impromptu exhibition that made our hair stand on end.

On getting to 'Filleted Phyllis' house we rolled up our greasy paper and each of us packed the paper as hard as we could into 'Filleted Phyllis' cast iron drainpipe, lit it and hid behind a facing wall. The drainpipe acted as a sort of wind tunnel and as the paper burned sent out an ever increasing WHOOSH that finished off with an ear splitting whistle. It made us jump the noise was so loud, and we were expecting it, I can only imagine the effect on the unsuspecting.

The whoosh and the whistle completed, Phyllis dashed out, in fact half a dozen doors came open, looking up at the skies one bloke was saying "What the chuffin ell were that?" another, "Ah thought bleedin Germans wa back."

We hid behind a wall peeking out and giggling, then 'Filleted Phyllis' confirmed that our trick had been successful by declaring, "It frightened the life outa me."

Schooldays in those days were so disciplined that you had to march in single file all the time, in most cases stick wielding teachers kept you in line at all times. The teachers seemed more interested in discipline and obedience that any academic results. So I suppose out of school we were sort of let loose.

Chapter 4

Turf Wars

As you will have realised my dad's brother Uncle Ern was a larger that life character. Ern lived nearby on Martin Lane. Although I enjoyed my visits to Uncle Ern's I always did so with some trepidation. Martin Lane was cobbled, as were most streets in that district. It had back-to-back houses on both sides. My Uncle Ern's house was situated at the far end of the lane.

On one of my first visits on my own aged about eight, I was walking down the middle of the lane, when to my left a head bobbed up. It was a lad about a couple of years older than me, he called out, "Hey what ya doin on here?" Before I could answer another had bobbed up about four feet away from the first one. I was staggered when the second boy said, "Argh what ya doin?" The thing that shook me up was the fact that both boys looked the same. They were in fact twins.

I later found out their names were Frank and Tony Hornsby. I had never seen twins before and it was a bit of a shock. The shock was about to get worse; I ought to have legged it straight away, but the shock of seeing twins for the first time caused me to freeze on the spot. Quick as a flash both Frank and Tony were over the wall. Each one grabbed hold of one of my hands and pulled it towards him. Then they both ran in a circle holding my arms stretched out, spinning me round for what seemed like an age. All of a sudden they let go of me. I was staggering towards Uncle Ern's like a drunken sailor. They both laughed at this, and then one kneed me in the thigh giving me the dead leg, so by now I was limping as I staggered on. Then for good measure they got an arm apiece and began twisting the skin in opposite directions (Indian burn). I struggled free and as I ran off they both started chucking bricks at me for good measure.

On arriving at Uncle Ern's I told him of my unpleasant experience. After staying a couple of hours or so at Uncle Ern's I asked him if he would walk me to the end of the lane. I didn't fancy a repeat performance from the twins. "Don't be daft," said Uncle Ern, "All yuv got to do is walk straight down't lane, then call ou, come on al feight ya both at once, then when they appear just give both of them a leathering." Ern's instructions were terrifying. As I set of I'd no intentions of carrying them out. As I reached the spot of the first attack by the twins I ran as fast as I could, I was back home in a flash.

I used to ask Dennis or Pete if they wanted to visit Ern's with me, they always declined by saying, "What un gu past twins house no chance." I suppose the twins act was territorial, it was a theme that ran right through the district.

Our archenemies on Martin Street were the Mushroom Lane gang. Mushroom Lane was situated on one side of the two playing areas known as the tip, whilst Martin Street was on the other side. Word was passed round one day that some half a dozen or so of the Mushroom Lane gang were playing football on the lower level of the tip. In no time we had a gang of about thirty. As we got to the tip we all pulled out great big grass sods from the grassy area that was on one side of the tip. We cornered the six kids and pelted them with the grass sods, covering them in muck before chasing them off.

Within a day or two word got round that some of the Mushroom Lane gang were on nearby Oxford Street. Within no time we had a gang together and up we went to Oxford Street. This time the Mushroom Lane Gang were the same in number as us about thirty. To the right on Oxford Street was a derelict bit of ground which stood up about six feet from the ground. As soon as we approached they began to pelt us with stones not grass sods. Despite having the Hornsby twins on our side we were on a loser. We had nothing to throw back so we had to wait while one of the opposite gang threw a brick, then one of our gang had to pick it up and throw it back. A couple of our gang got hit, one, I remember, just over the eye. Each kid that was hit ran off crying, much to the amusement of the Mushroom Lane kids.

Someone must have reported the disturbance, because all of a sudden a police car came roaring up with its bell clanging out. The police car pulled up with a jerk and out popped four policemen running around trying to grab hold of any kid within reach. It was probably like trying to grab a piece of wet soap. Within no time at all, the sixty or so kids had scattered.

We ran off towards Martin Street. Once on top of Martin Street, we had the cellar grate off the first house we came to. Pete, Dennis and I slid down the cellar. Pete had placed the cellar grate back in place so that no one would be the wiser. We looked up with bated breath through the holes in the cellar grate to see a policeman with hands on his hips, he said out loud to another policeman, "Wer've all't chuffin kids gone?" There obviously wasn't a kid in sight. The other policeman answered by asking a question, "What do ya reckon, a bit of house to house enquiries?" "Are ya joking," answered the policeman, "Have ya ever done house to house round here? Its three monkeys' job, seen nowt, say nowt, heard nowt. Come on we'd better bugger off, we wasting argh time round here."

As soon as we heard their footsteps disappear we were back up the cellar grate and off home. My dad was reading the evening paper; I slipped in and sat at the table, head in the palms of my hand elbows on table.

My dad suddenly chimes up, "Hey what about this?" he says to my mother. Quoting from 'The Star' he says, "Police Inspector somebody or other says people have been heard laughing and whistling on Crookesmoor Road as late as 10 o'clock, the Inspector went on to say such behaviour would not be tolerated and will be stamped out." My mother replied, "Don't know what world's comin too." I gulped silently thinking compared to grown ups talking and whistling at 10 o'clock I wonder what Chief Inspector thought of kids chucking bricks at each other at 7 o'clock.

Next morning at assembly our head teacher was accompanied by a policeman on one side and at the other side by our teacher holding his cane. The policeman gave the rough gist of what went on, and then the head said, "If any of you were involved please indicate by raising your hand." Needless to say not one hand went up. As for me, I was wondering what the punishment would have been, our teacher would give you the cane for sneezing. If that was a guideline chucking stones at each other could only be a punishment of hanging or garrotting.

The peculiar thing about it was that kids from Mushroom Lane and Martin Street would mix together at school, no problem. So I suppose the stone chucking exercise was some sort of release and indeed territorial.

Chapter 5

Big Derek

Getting on the bus one day, sometime in the nineties, I couldn't believe my eyes. I asked the driver, "Are you called Derek?" He nodded without a trace of interest in my question. "Did you go to Crookesmoor School?" I pried further. "Argh," he snapped back countering with, "O tha gerrin ont bus o what?"

He had no interest whatsoever in my questions so I paid my fare and found a seat. Derek must have been having a bad day, so it was never going to be a back slapping, "How ya going on," occasion. I got off with a, "See ya Derek." Derek looked away, it must have been fifty years or so since I last saw him, yet incredibly Derek had not changed that much. I was pleased for Derek, for I was sure he had got the job of his dreams, or judging by his demeanour was getting fed up with it.

Derek was a couple of years older than me. I must have been about eight years old and Derek ten. But that's where the similarity of any kind ended. I was tall and skinny for a kid, as for Derek he was built like a man, a freakish build for a ten year old. He had big thick arms, huge hands, and feet. He used to wear long trousers, which for a ten year old was unusual in those days. Looking at him as a kid I thought if he carried on growing at the same rate, he'd be 15 foot 10 by the time he was twenty. At ten years old Derek was wearing men's cloths. I swear he must have only grown six inches in the last fifty years.

Another unusual thing about Derek was that he always carried a big biscuit tin lid under his arm. I never saw Derek with out it. For his passion was for buses. Every playtime he used to fill his imaginary bus with imaginary petrol, from an imaginary petrol pump. He would then fill his used milk bottle full of water and pour it into an imaginary radiator. The fact that the water would simply go on the playground floor didn't spoil the illusion for Derek. He would then stand with his biscuit tin lid held in both hands, he always removed one hand to adjust his imaginary mirror, and then he was ready for off, making loud, "BRRRUM, BRRRUM," noises as he went.

While all this was going on all the other kids would hide away because Derek used to like all of the other kids to join in as passengers. There was always a teacher on playground duty, whoever the teacher was would look on bemused by Derek's actions and also by the fact that all the other kids seemed to have vanished. 'Bar' for Derek and his bus, the playground was like a ghost town. However it didn't put Derek off.

Away he went looking for passengers, "BRRRUM, BRRRUM," noises coming from him, turning his tin lid as though a steering wheel. "Ave seen ya," he'd shout at kids hidden behind a pillar, "Ger on," and they would form a line of twos behind Derek, and off he'd go searching for more passengers. He wouldn't be satisfied until he'd got ten pairs of kids behind him. Pete and I were to fall victim, "Ah can see thi Passy, n thee n all Marshall, come on ger'ron."

Every time he stopped we had to run on the spot while he picked up more passengers. "Me feet o killin me," Pete complained at one no request stop. Pete had his usual hob nail boots on. As for me, I was lucky, I had my usual black slippers on, and so compared to Pete I was in clover. Off we went with Derek, "BRRRUM, BRRRUMING," to his hearts content, up steps round pillars, down steps every inch covered. All us kids jogging on behind, round and round, up and down; Derek would turn his wheel and start to go slower, then all of a sudden there'd be a louder, "BRRRUM, BRRRUM," and off he'd dash with all of us red faced and knackered trying to keep up.

All of a sudden one day he stopped, pulled up his imaginary hand brake and climbed out of his imaginary cab. He ordered us to keep running on the spot as he pointed out that he had not switched the engine off. With his hands on hips, his biscuit tin lid under his arm he bellowed, "Ya not talking. Ya should be talking, like passengers do," so with a, "Don't forget, talk," he climbed back into his imaginary cab and away we went "BRRRUM, BRRRUM." Derek looked over his shoulder and shouted back at us, "Come on chuffin talk." I turned my head and said to Pete as ordered, "Turned chilly an it?" Pete replied, "Chilly! Its worse than't foreign legion I'm knackered."

The teacher would bring our bus to a halt, signalling the end of dinnertime by blowing his whistle. Derek as calm as you like would put his tin lid under his arm and then get in line to return to his class. I whispered to

45

Pete, "He's bus driving mad." Pete replied, "Am glad he dunt think he's Donald Campbell!" One day, after being on what seemed like a seventy mile bus journey, we returned to class only for the teacher to announce, "Right you boys who's for P.E.?"

One day news reached the playground that there was going to be a gang war with the Mushroom Lane gang after school at the nearby tip. All the kids off Martin Street would converge on the tip picking up stones or owt else that thi could chuck. We would look up and see the Mushroom Lane gang on the horizon all armed with sticks and stones. It was like a scene from the cowboy films as all the Mushroom Lane gang came rushing down the banking yelping and hollering like Apaches.

Derek must have been passing for he came dashing across from the right side of the tip with his biscuit tin under his arm. He must have seen all the kids and thought, loads o passengers. The gangs were about fifteen yards apart, Derek ran between each gang shouting, "Do ya wanna game o buses?"

The tip was cleared in minutes. I was off with Pete saying, "He can fuck off." Derek's reputation must have gone before him because the Mushroom Lane gang disappeared just as quickly.

I think that Derek only stayed at Crookesmoor for about six months. If he'd stayed longer I'm sure Crookesmoor would have produced many a long distance runner due to Derek's bus journeys. One day I said to Pete, "Seems funny without Derek dun it? Does tha miss him?" Pete replied, "Argh like I'd miss a broken leg."

Chapter 6

Here comes Summer

Summer in 1950 for a little kid meant six weeks off school. These six weeks seemed long and boring. Hot days, at times sitting around the house staring at flypaper hung up on our ceiling and hanging down by the side of a single light bulb. Chin on hand, elbow on table, I'd sit staring at the flypaper trying to count the dead flies.

I always got on my mother's nerves during the six weeks holidays. I'd sometimes address her before thinking what I was going to ask. This got any conversation off on the wrong foot. She'd be busy black leading the fireplace.

Me: "Mam"
Mother: "What?" (Whilst carrying on working).
Me: "Mam"
Mother: "WHAAAT?" (Exploding into a temper).
Me: "Av nowt to do."
Mother: "Get out an play with Dennis Aistrop."
Me: "Wiv fell arght."
Mother: "Well fall back in again."
Me: "Mother."
Mother: "What? What? What?"
Me: "Canna av a penny?"
Mother: "Canna av this? Canna av that? We aught to have called you Canna, no you can't."
Me: "Why?"

Mother: "Cuz ya can't, ya must think I'm made a money. Stop chuffin mytherin, Canna have a penny? (Said mockingly) kids today thi don't know thi born. Get out of me sight before a lose me temper."

There was a knock on our door, "O ya comin out to play?" asked Pete Marshall, "Ave got some handcuffs that mi uncle bought me. Me and Dennis o goin ont tip." The falling out with Dennis was soon forgotten and next thing we were heading off to the tip, Pete, Dennis and myself complete with a pair of toy handcuffs.

Dennis looked a bit odd, he was wearing his usual raggy arsed trousers, and his well worn peeped toe shoes, but he was also wearing a big fawn coloured bush hat that his uncle had brought home from Burma.

Dennis had an idea. He said he knew a big yard that was full of old tyres on St. Philips Road, and that it would be easy to pinch one. What we would do with it when we got it did not come into the equation. It would be better than counting flies on flypaper.

We got to St. Philips Road, and sure enough Dennis was spot on, a huge yard full of old tyres. The big gate on the yard was ajar. A big lorry tyre was stood up on its edge; we were soon rolling it up St. Philips Road, on to Barber Road in the direction of the tip. It's a miracle no policeman saw us, what with Dennis wearing the oversized bush hat and the three of us rolling a four foot tyre complete with steel inset.

We got to the tip and rested the tyre on the railings. Suddenly Dennis spotted a lad of our age come from the Mushroom Lane area and start to walk down the long winding steps towards the tip. Dennis said, "Let's gerim, eez one at Mushroom Lane gang." So the three of us surrounded him in no time, and using Pete's handcuffs, handcuffed him to some railings behind a bush. When we interrogated him he told us he was meeting up with his pals on the banking overlooking the tip.

We crawled through the grass and looked down the banking to see about ten kids trying to get a fire started. "Mushroom Lane gang", Dennis whispered. We backtracked to our tyre; all of a sudden we'd found a use for it. The three of us rolled it on the top edge till we were looking down onto the Mushroom Lane gang. They had got the fire well and truly burning like a big bonfire. All the kids were dancing round it laughing. Pete said they looked like Apaches.

At the top of the banking we took aim and let the tyre go rolling down in the direction of the gang. The tyre quickly gathered momentum, bouncing down gathering more and more pace, as it did so we suddenly realised it would probably do some real damage if it hit anybody. At the last second we all shouted, "Watch out," the gang looked up then quickly jumped to safety. The tyre crashed through the fire, sending embers all over. Then the gang of about ten started running up the banking after us, being ten kids after three we split up and dashed off in different directions.

I fell into the house, startling my mother in the process.

Mother: "What the chuffin ell?" she went on, "What ya been up to?"
Me: "Nowt."
Mother: "Ya outa breath."
Me: "Wiv been havin a race."
Mother: "With who?"
Me: "Dennis an Pete."
Mother: "Well ya racings over mi lad, ya stop in this house o ya listening?"

We had our tea, it must have been 7:30pm or later. I was listening to 'Dick Barton Special Agent' on the wireless. In the programme Dick Barton said to his sidekick, "Have you got the handcuffs?"

Handcuffs, lightning struck my brain. In all the kafuffle we had left the kid handcuffed to the railings, for what now would be about two hours. I jumped up and made for the door. "Where do ya think your goin?" queried my mam. "Just to lav," I replied.

I quickly dashed across the yard to Pete's, I asked him out, then said, "We've left that kid handcuffed to railings." Pete shocked me by saying, "Oh well gu tommora." I persuaded him we couldn't leave him there all night. So along with Dennis we went up the tip to release our prisoner.

We heard him before we saw him, he was shouting,

"MAM, MAM." Dennis took control, getting the keys off Pete he undid the handcuffs saying to the kid, "Don't ever mess with the Martin Street gang." The lad nodded in approval and dashed off in the direction of Mushroom Lane. Once out of catching distance he began shouting obscenities at us, then disappeared.

We took the shortest route back, which was straight down Martin Street. We noticed a crowd gathered. We pushed our way through the crowd to see a policeman taking notes; there was a big black car with a huge dent in it, and by its side, a big lorry tyre. We slipped away as the policeman said to the car owner, "Well doctor we will make extensive enquiries."

I got back into the house to face my mother.
Mother: "Where have you been?"
Me: "Tut lav."
Mother: "What for an hour?"
Me: "Had got stomach ache."
Mother: "Well ya stayin in tomorra, an he'll (me dad) get to know about this lot."

The summer of 1950 became most memorable because of my mothers sister, Auntie May. Auntie May was a spinster, and at the time lived with my granddad on Whitehouse Lane. In fact she lived with him until his death. Auntie May was always a welcome visitor to our house in Martin Street, because she never came empty handed, always a comic or a few sweets.

This particular day was to prove the most exciting. After a whispered confab with my mother she asked me, "How would you like to go with me to Blackpool for the week?" I was speechless for a while, "Blackpool for a week." It seemed unbelievable. "Oh yes," I shouted. "That's it then," replied May, we're off in a couple of weeks.

Up till then the only time I'd been to the seaside was a visit to Cleethorpes, thanks to Radford Street Working Men's Club. Blackpool for a whole week seemed a million miles from Martin Street. Auntie May explained that my cousin Marlene would be going as well, Marlene was Auntie May's brother Tom's girl. As she left the house she said, "Don't forget to be a good lad for ya mam, or you'll not be goin."

So for two weeks I hardly slept, and hardly stepped a foot outside our house. Everything was, "Yes mam, no mam," to such an extent I think it began to get on my mother's nerves. Dennis would call to ask my mam, "Iz your Fred comin arght to play?" My mother would look at me and say, "Well?" I'd reply, "No." My mother would send Dennis off with, "He says he's not coming out." I daren't risk the chance of being involved in any sort of trouble. My self-imposed imprisonment in our house really got on my mother's nerves. She would say, "If I see much more of you just staring at four walls, al gu round bend." To which I obediently replied, "Yes mam", which only seemed to get her madder.

It soon came round to Blackpool time. Auntie May,

Marlene and myself left for Blackpool by train from Sheffield Victoria railway station, an added excitement for me, for up till then I'd never been on a train. As we pulled in at Blackpool station my heart was in my mouth at the first sight of Blackpool Tower.

As we got off the train we were approached by young lads of my age, who were offering to take you to your digs. We placed our cases in the lads wheelbarrow, Auntie May told him the address, and off we went following the lad. I suppose he was a sort of working class, non motoring kind of taxi. On arrival at our digs, I think the lad charged six pence, wished us a good holiday, and then scampered off back to the station for a new customer.

As food was on ration Auntie May brought a suitcase full of food. The house we stayed at was just a private house. We had use of the front bedroom, and front living room. Before leaving the house in the morning, Auntie May would give the lady of the house the food to prepare for when we got back.

Our first port of call was the shops. Auntie May bought me a flannel, a sponge, a plastic soap dish, a toothbrush and toothpaste. The toothpaste was in a round tin; it came in two colours, pink for girls, and in my case blue. Whenever I used it, it was like polishing your teeth with peppermint flavoured grit.

On the Sunday we spent our time on the sands, and Auntie May went into the details of our timetable for the week. On the next day she said we would go to all the theatres and book our places for the shows, I could hardly contain myself at the thought of seeing stars who I'd only heard previously on the wireless.

The shows we booked were singer Josef Locke, the play 'Hobson's Choice' starring Wilfred Pickles, Donald Peers the singer, and my favourite comedian Al Read, who was performing on the pier. To see these people in the flesh seemed truly unbelievable. Josef Locke finished his show singing 'Goodbye, goodbye I wish you all the luck, goodbye' to tremendous applause. I was amazed to see Wilfred Pickles emerge from a trap door in 'Hobson's Choice', and Al Read brought the house down on the pier. I had sore hands from clapping.

When watching the singer Donald Peers, I witnessed for the first time a heckler. As Donald Peers began to sing his hit 'By a Babbling Brook', a bloke at the front of the audience called out, "Ya can't sing," Donald stopped for a few seconds, and then began to carry on. When the bloke again shouted, " That rubbish tha can't sing," Donald signalled for the orchestra to stop, saying to the heckler, "Can't sing Eh," then going on, "I'll have you know if I lose my voice I will receive ten thousand pounds in insurance," to which the heckler replied, "What did ya spend the money on? Cuz ya thas lost it." Some of the audience started laughing, then two blokes arrived and escorted the heckler out of the theatre, still he shouted, "Ah want mi money back that rubbish." Donald very coolly went on to finish his 'By a Babbling Brook'. As for his singing, as a little kid, I was, I suppose, on the hecklers side.

Whilst at Blackpool we also visited the fun house, a big hall with all sorts of contraptions. You paid your money and you had to enter by a series of obstacles, over a moving staircase, through a revolving barrel. Finally over a space that kept blasting jets of air upwards blowing the females dresses up, all in front of cinema style seats full of blokes.

In front of the Fun House was a huge model of a clown in a glass box laughing all the time really loud. I was intrigued by one of the side stalls. It had model clowns heads with mouths wide open, the heads moved from side to side and you would pay to drop table tennis balls in their mouth. The balls would then drop down into a tray with separate compartments, and if your balls were received over a number you would win some small prize.

Whilst walking on Blackpool front one day there was a bloke calling out, "Come and see 'Syncopating Sandy' as he attempts to break the world non-stop piano playing marathon." Outside was a big blackboard and on it was written 34 hours. Auntie May said, "Come on we'll find this interesting." As we queued the bloke rubbed out the 34 hours and replaced it with 35 hours. As we shuffled in we saw Sandy sitting at his piano, his coat draped over the back of the chair he was on, sleeves rolled up, trilby propped on the back of his head, big blue braces, and a cigarette in his mouth. Old Sandy looked shattered. He was separated from his audience by a roped off area. For effect, I suppose, there were two steel oxygen bottles. There were also two St. John Ambulance Brigade people, a stretcher, a bucket, and on the piano three ashtrays full of tab ends. We shuffled off out into the sunlight.

A big poster outside read:
'World Champion
Every Day 9am til 5pm
Except Sunday'

I went away wondering if he carried on after 5pm or indeed Sundays.

We visited Blackpool Tower and heard Reginald Dixon playing his organ, Auntie May told us that Reginald was in fact a Sheffielder. We also saw a big mangy lion in what looked like a very small cage; I came away feeling sorry for the lion. I'd had such a good time, when it came to leaving Blackpool I had a lump in my throat at the prospect of returning to reality back in Martin Street.

When I eventually returned to school, I sat daydreaming, staring blankly out of the window, wondering to myself, "I wonder if 'Syncopating Sandy' is still playing his piano." I was abruptly brought out of my daydream by the teacher calling out, "Pass pay attention," he ordered me to the front of the class. He then demanded me to tell him what I was thinking about. I answered, "Syncopating Sandy." He obviously did not know who Sandy was, gave me the cane and told me to pay attention in future, adding "You read too many comics Pass."

One barmy summer's day we were sitting on the pavement steps opposite from our entry, there was Jenks, Dennis, Pete and myself, we'd been playing film stars. Three would stand on one side of the road; whoever was 'on' would stand on the other and call out the initials of a famous film star. The other three had to guess the film star. A wrong guess meant the person who was on could jump into the middle of the road. When someone guessed correctly, it was a race to see who could reach the opposite side first. So if your opponent's guess was wrong you had a start over them.

If it sounds a bit gormy and naff it's because it probably was. A woman on the road got fed up with the noise we created and in no uncertain terms told us to clear off. The woman in question was none other than Mrs 'Miserable Get' as we nicknamed her. This was the same woman who had confiscated our ball. It wouldn't have been so bad but the only reason we were playing film stars was because we had no ball, she'd still got it. So we were reduced to sitting, moping, and bored out of our minds. We had pleaded in the past for our ball, it fell on deaf ears. We'd posted a load of moggies down her cellar grate for retribution, but nothing would ever get our ball back. Mrs 'Miserable Get' was a dead ringer of the character that was often portrayed in films by Peggy Mount, only louder and tougher. I don't think she was capable of smiling.

Anyway there we were all four of us sitting opposite Mrs 'Miserable Get's,' bored out of our minds. All of a sudden Dennis says, "Ey up," and nods in the direction of a bloke making his way up Martin Street in our direction. The bloke, despite it being a very hot summer's day, was wearing a gabardine mac open at the front, the belt of the mac was almost trailing on the floor, perched on the back of his head was a trilby. Straight away I thought a collector, or a salesman, due to the fact he was carrying a huge suitcase, I knew it had to be the latter. For any collector on Martin Street would not have needed a suitcase for money. We noticed he stopped intermittently, knocking on doors that were slammed in his face.

As he got opposite us he put his suitcase down, and strolled over in our direction. He was blood red in the face and was sweating profusely due to a combination of the weather, the suitcase, and his salesman's uniform of mac and trilby. He greeted us with, "Hi ya lads," he went on, "Do ya want to ern a tanner?" None of us answered, he persisted, "Am selling encyclopaedias, if you direct me to someone who likes reading thiz a tanner in it for ya." I thought to myself, "He'd have more chance selling chandeliers than encyclopaedias on Martin Street!"

Three of us were shaking our heads when Dennis dives in to say, "I know someone." "Who?" asks the salesman. Dennis bargains, "You said you'd give us a tanner." The salesman digs into his pocket and flicks a tanner to Dennis with the question, "Who then?" Dennis then points to the house opposite, Mrs 'Miserable Get's'. "What's their name?" says the salesman and quick as a flash Dennis answered, "Mrs. Shishpot" "Shishpot?" says the salesman, "Funny name in it?" Dennis replies, "Well that's her name." Her name was nothing like Shishpot but we can see what Dennis is up to, we are almost strangling ourselves to suppress laughter. "Thanks young un," says the salesman as he walks over to Mrs 'Miserable Get's'.

He puts his case down on the pavement straightens his tie, repositions his trilby, sort of shrugs his shoulders then knocks. We are all waiting with bated breath. We didn't have to wait long. He had hardly finished knocking when the door sprang open. In a loud voice the fearsome Mrs 'Miserable Get' demanded, "What?" "Ho," says the salesman clearly taken aback by the sight of Mrs 'Miserable Get'. He then stutters on, "Good afternoon Mrs. Shishpot can I interest you in an encyclopaedia?" Mrs 'Miserable Get' was wearing a pinny and a sort of blouse with the sleeves rolled up to her arm pits. "Ya cheeky bugger ger off chuffin street before ah do ya some damage," then she steps aggressively towards the salesman who has now grabbed his suitcase and is doing his best to run away.

Because of his suitcase he is running with a sort of limp, while being pursued by Mrs 'Miserable Get'. We were rolling about laughing. Due to the commotion three or four doors opened. All enquiring what was going on? "Ah don't know what world's coming to," declares Mrs 'Miserable Get'. She goes on to the gathering crowd, "Knocks on mi door wanting to sell mi encyclopaedias, then calls mi Mrs. 'Shitpot', ave never erd out like it, cheeky chuff, al geeim some Mrs. 'Shitpot', if ah ever see him round here again." She had translated Mrs. 'Shishpot' into Mrs. 'Shitpot'. From that day we dropped the nickname Mrs 'Miserable Get', we all preferred her new name, Mrs. 'Shitpot'.

Chapter 7

Making do and mending

They say necessity is the mother of invention; well that was certainly the case in Martin Street in the 40s and early 50s. One morning before setting off to school I complained that holes had appeared in the soles of each of my shoes. "Lets 'ave a look," said my dad. After inspecting them he handed them to my mother with the words, "Put some cardboard in them an' I'll sort em out at weekend." My mother didn't answer but duly obliged my dad's request. Her frown and indeed her silence suggested that she was not exactly over the moon with his comments.

Come the weekend my dad announced, "I'm off tut market for some leather soles, al fix Fred's shoes when ah get back." My mother answered rather tentatively, "Ad be better teken um tut cobblers." "Cobblers," replied me dad, "Cost a fortune, n besides wiv got a perfectly good hobbin-foot int cellar doin nowt." Hobbinfoots were a steel contraption with three legs at the end of each leg was a foot shape, each shape was a different size, you placed the shoe that needed mending on the appropriate foot and you had a base on which you could do your cobbling.

On returning from town my dad proudly held up a brown paper bag and said, "Look at this lot, a bag full of leather soles all fo a tanner," he went on, "An you say gu tut cobblers." In a flash he 'fetched' up the hobbin-foot from the cellar, he sat crossed legged on the floor and armed with a hammer and nails began hammering one of the newly acquired leather soles on to one of my shoes.

I stood shoeless by my mother's side. Her silence spoke volumes. It was obvious by her silence that she wasn't exactly full of confidence in my dad's cobbling skills. "Nah then," my dad declared, "That's soon on." My mother broke her silence by saying, "It's too big." Her limited comment suggested what she was really thinking was he's gonna make a cock up of it. "Course it's too big," my dad snapped back, "Ya have tu pare them down to size with a knife.

"Wiv not got a cobblers knife," again a comment using the minimum of words. Her short interruptions agitated my dad, "Shut up," he said, "Wiv got summat just az good." He went to the sideboard drawer and pulled out our one and only carving knife, "Not sharp enough," my mother said tersely. "Will be soon," growled me dad. I could sense a volcano about to erupt. My dad took the carving knife and began scraping it on our step in an effort to sharpen it. "Ah cut bread wi that," commented my arms folded mother. My dad didn't reply but was beginning to bite his lip.

He began paring down the leather to the size of my shoe in complete post-volcano eruption silence. The silence was broken by Dennis Aistrop popping his head round our door asking, "Are ya coming to play football Fred?" My mother intercepted my intended answer by saying, "No love, he can't yet," there was a short pause then slowly she added, "Iz dads mending iz shoes." She said those last five words like a judge would send someone to the gallows. We had a mini eruption, "Just shut it," snapped my dad, repeating, "Just shut it, ah tha listenin?" My mother looked on with a stone faced silence. "Ah, that's one done," my dad announced, "Pass me another sole," he said to my mother. My mother delved into the paper bag and pulled out the remaining leather soles. "Where did ya buy um from?" asked my mother, "Market." "Neer mind were ah gorrem from just pass us a chuffin sole," said my dad.

"There all different thickness and sizes," said my mother, "Don't tell me tha didn't check em first. That one yuv put on's abarght a quarter inch thick some of these o'like wafers." "Course a checked em what do ya expect fo a tanna?" His slightly hesitant reply suggested he hadn't checked them.

My mother turned her head to one side and out of the corner of her mouth said, "A tanner chucked int street." "What were that? What tha sayin?" barked me dad getting madder all the time.

Dennis, who I'd not noticed must have sensed an impending eruption and still had his head around our door whilst still standing outside. He must have been there a couple of minutes despite my mother answering to the negative on his asking, "Are ya coming to play football Fred?" My dad noticed this and Dennis got both barrels, "Ah thar still here Aistrop piss off." My dad was unloading a much needed load of laver.

"Just pass me two soles," he ordered my mother.

He soon had them on the other shoe, paired them down, then proudly declared, "Job done." He passed my mother the carving knife; she stared at the blade slowly shaking her head before putting it back into our sideboard drawer.

"Nah then Fred lad try these on." His cutting down to size with the carving knife was not exactly a work of art each shoe was a quarter of an inch wider, plus the fact that the shoes were black and my new soles were beige, meant that they had a sort of clown like appearance.

As I tried them on my mother was about to speak when my dad stepped in pointing his finger at her, "Just shut it, don't you say a chuffin word, ah tha listnin? Not one word." After I got them on he asked, "Come on Fred what do ya think?" "Smashin," I lied. I wasn't about to become responsible for 'War of the Worlds'. "There ya gu," my dad announced, "Saved us a fortune." Judge Gladys Pass declined to comment.

Next day I decided, deliberately, to go to school with Dennis. For no matter how clown like my shoes were, I would look relatively well dressed compared to poor old Dennis. My dad had put new soles on my shoes but not new heels, as a result when walking my heel would touch the floor then my foot would snap as my sole hit the pavement. Due to the fact that the soles of my mended shoes were thicker than the heels made I felt I was walking uphill; plus the fact that one sole was thicker than the other meant that I walked with a permanent limp.

So Dennis and I were off to school, Dennis in his toeless shoes, raggy arsed and no underpants under his trousers, and me in my black coloured beige trimmed, uphill walking limp-a-long shoes.

On reaching the playground before lessons began, the inevitable happened. "What tha limpin at Passy? Tha looks like thaz stood on two fishcakes." All sorts of comments followed, it all got out of hand quickly. The result was I ended up rolling about on the playground floor with one of my tormenters. A teacher pulled us apart and ordered that we report ourselves outside the headmaster's study after assembly.

We waited outside the head's room with some trepidation. Our teacher would dish the stick out but being sent to the head meant big league punishment. I knocked on the door, "ENTER," bellowed out the head and in we went. As we approached his desk the head didn't look up but continued writing something or other. My sparring partner was a lad called Bobby Vickers, a tiny lad compared to me, being small was probably a mental stipulation of mine before getting into a fight. Bobby was just like the rest of us and in reality was a pal of mine. If the boot had been on the other foot, or to be more specific the shoe, I'd have been taking the mickey out of him.

The head stood pulling down the ends of his waistcoat as he did so, ready to do the business. "You know full well," he pontificated, "Brawling and unseemly behaviour will not be tolerated in my school." He emphasised the 'My' as an indication of power. He looked down on Bobby and said, "What's your name?" Bobby replied, "Vickers sir," his voice was a couple of octaves higher than usual, probably due to fear.

My heart was pounding as I thought, "Chuffin ell Bobby sounds like Jimmy Clitheroe." "...and you boy?" "Pass," I replied. "Well Pass, go over and fetch my stick." His stick was hung on the wall by two brass hooks, displayed for all to see. As for fetching the stick and handing it over to a bloke who was about to hit you with it, it added humiliation to the punishment. Due to my newly cobbled shoes I limped over, got the stick and handed it the head.

He looked a bit taken aback with my walking impediment and asked, "Why are you limping Pass?" "Ah fell darn last week when ah wo doin some shoppin fo an old lady up ah street." It sounded good and besides that I knew the truth never worked with teachers. "Oh I see," said the head in sort of a mind blowing sympathetic sort of way. "Were gonna gera way with it," flashed through my mind. "Am sorry fo fighting," I lied. "It weren't his fault," I said meaning Bobby, "It were all my fault."

So with my puritanical ways of helping old people, (not true), plus Bobby's Jimmy Clitheroe impression, the headmaster's hard exterior began to melt. "Well boys," said the head, "you know you should not fight in the school grounds don't you. I don't ever want to see you here again, understand? Put my stick back Pass and off you go back to your class." I returned his stick back on the hooks of the wall, and left his office with a more profound limp than ever. The exaggerated limp was just thrown in for good measure.

On returning from school that day my dad asked how I'd got on with my shoes. I told him of the limp they had caused and he replied that he would cobble another sole to level them up when he'd got time at the weekend. My mother's total silence spoke volumes. I was thinking if he carries on adding soles to my shoes I'll be the only six foot ten, eight year old at Crookesmoor School.

I returned home from school the next day and asked my mam, "Weerz me dad?" "He's doin a double un," she replied. A 'double un' meant a sixteen hour shift instead of the normal eight hour shift. She turned, then added, "Try these on," handing me a pair of black slippers. As I took off my shoes, which looked like a couple of small canal barges, my mother chucked each one on the fire without comment. When I finally saw my dad he never mentioned cobbling, he must have thought pack up while you're losing.

A bone of contention for my mother was the state of our table, it had at one time been a polished affair, but it had seen better days. It was covered in scratches, which was not helped by the fact that my brother Brian and I used to play 'shove apney' on it.

When my mam and dad weren't in we would nail two imaginary goalposts at each end of the table and play a sort of football game. Each player would have a penny that represented your team and the ball would be a halfpenny. You each took turns in shoving your penny against the halfpenny in an effort to score a goal between the nail goalposts. Hence the name 'shove apney'. (The 'apney' being a dialect of halfpenny.)

The fact that my mother never complained about our antics explained the condition of the table, it was beyond restitution. It was always covered, except on wash days, by a table cloth.

Bonfire night 1951 brought about a change, my dad's younger brother Ernest arrived to announce, "Come and gee us a lift Fred, ave got somat fo ya." They both disappeared up our entry and both came back down with a huge, obviously second hand, farmhouse sort of table. "Wiz tha got that from?" said my mother, adding, "It's too high." My Uncle Ern deflected her question with the words, "Oh ah just come across it," as though everybody was falling over tables every day.

Our previous table was put out in the yard, and the replacement put in its place. "It's too high," reiterated my mother. "Sit tut table," she told me, with the size of our chairs when I was sitting it was eye level to me, to eat at it would be for me like eating over a high wall. "See," said my mother. "No problem," bailed in my dad, "just wants a couple of inches off each leg."

"Thiz better news," interrupted Ern. "Come on Fred," he said to my dad, "Ge us another lift." They both disappeared again to the lorry of one of Ern's mates who was delivering the table as a favour. Out of the cab of the lorry Ern unloaded four crates of brown ale. "What could be better?" exclaimed Ern, "New table owd un ont bonfire, well be sat round it wi a bottle of beer in uz hands."

The old table was quickly smashed up quick sticks,

me dad was good at smashing things up. Armed with his saw he soon had a couple of inches, roughly off the four legs of our newly acquired piece of furniture. One problem when my dad pressed his hand down on the table it rocked. "Nah then," said Ern, "Ya might have to do a bit more sawing to level it up." "Let's have a think," he said passing my dad a bottle of brown ale, then opening one himself, "Ah lets ave a think."

My mother said, "Ya no you two, it's any excuse for a booze up." To which Ernest replied lifting his bottle of beer, "I'll drink to that." My dad burst out laughing at this. Ernest went on, "Duz tha kno Fred my eyes o getting worse, av beed tut opticians today and guess who I bumped into?" "Who?" asked me dad. "Everybody," replied Ern, causing more laughter, this infuriated my mother more. "Come on," my mother said to me, "Come on, get ya coat on." "Were ya goin?" questioned me dad. "To our May's," said my mother. May was mother's sister who lived within walking distance.

As we went up our entry my mother muttered to herself, "Lets ave a think, more like lets ave a drink." Then looked down at me saying, "Wi better off out of it." We spent a couple of hours or so at Aunt May's. It was starting to go dusk as we returned to our yard. Our old table, in pieces, sat proudly on top of the bonfire that was situated in the centre of the yard. I was relieved to see that they had not lit the bonfire yet.

From our house came a distant singing of 'If ya Irish come into the parlour.' "Ah knew it," said my mother, "Ah bloody well knew it." As we entered our house we both got the shock of our lives, the table had been reduced to one that was about eighteen inches from the floor. My dad and Ern were sitting on the floor surrounded by empty beer bottles.

My dad greeted my mother with, "Ey up love argh ya goin?" "Arghm a goin? What the chuffin ell's that?" nodding in the direction of the table. Ern chimed up, "Thi ave em (hick) like this in China (hick) argh chuffin mad abarht um like (hick) this in China." My dad who was oblivious of my mother's expression burst out laughing, "Owd Ern wiv ad a reight neet, ampt wi, argh a reight neet." Stern faced mother said, "And what wi gonna do fo a table? That looks like it's been made fot seven dwarfs." They both laughed out loud at my mother's comments.

Ern, noticing my mother's dour expression, staggered to his feet and said, "Oh it looks as though you're in trouble Fred lad, am off orm." "So long," said my dad, "See ya tumorra." As Ernest disappeared my mother carried on with her original question, "And what wi gonna do now for a table?" "I'm off to bed," said my dad, adding, "Tha worries too much somat'll turn up. Ge us a shout int mouning about half past five."

As soon as my dad was upstairs my mother sprang into action, dragging the table outside, "Give me a lift Beet," she called out to Mrs. Aistrop and between them put our new table on the bonfire.

Everyone came out of their respective houses and sat round in their straight backed chairs as the fire was lit. As the flickering fire gained momentum I asked, "What

70

we gonna do for a table mam?" "Ya better gu and ask him, 'chuffin andyman' (me dad)." All us kids were dancing round the fire, big potatoes were put on the fire which tasted delicious when smothered in butter.

Everybody's fireworks were used up in no time. Dennis Aistrop's dad put on his usual impromptu display by packing each house's drainpipe with paper then lighting it. WHOOSH, WHOOSH, WHOOSH, WHOOSH, WHOOSH, WHOOSH, and finally WHOOSH. It sounded like a replay of the Second World War.

The women sat nattering, while the kids ran round playing, which seemed well into the night. As they say, a good time was had by one and all, though you would not have thought so by my mother's expression.

The next day my dad had his tea presented to him on the floor by his feet, I had mine on my knee whilst sat on our step. We had to eat like that for a couple of days. I came home from school one day to find out we had another table. When I asked where it came from, "Ya Uncle Erns dropped it off," answered my non-smiling mother.

A couple of weeks later I went on a visit to my Uncle Ern's with my dad. They were laughing recalling the table caper. My dad asked, "It were a big chuffin table Ern, where did ya get it from?" Uncle Ern's reply scared the life out of me when he answered, "Ah know a bloke who works fo Tomlinson's he gave me a few bob to get rid of it for him. A put a few bob to it and bought ale." The key word to me was Tomlinson's, they were the local undertaker. My dad was taken aback by Ern's answer saying, "Chuffin

Tomlinson's, that's why it wu so high. What did thi use it fo, weshin bodies down o what?" Ern replied in a matter of fact manner, "Probably." "Blimey," said me dad, "Just as well it ended up were it did." My dad looked down on me and said, "Not one word to her (my mother) o ya listin?" He confronted Ern again saying, "What tha dooin bringing a chuffin table frompt morgue?" "Thaz got to make do and mend Fred lad, make do and mend."

As you will have realised my dad was a sort of 'Don't do it yourself' kinda bloke, but as for working hard, he could not have been bettered. 'Bar' for breaking his leg when I was about six I never knew him to miss a day's work. The only time after that was when cancer dragged him down at the age of 63. As for me being a handyman, I would say my dad was marginally better.

Chapter 8

A trip upstairs

My mother interrupted me from a game of marbles I was having with Pete and Dennis. She thrust a note and some money in my hand and a shopping bag in the other. I shot off towards our entry only to be reminded, "And don't forget to call at Mrs. Smith's."

It was a reminder that I didn't want to hear, for Mrs. Smith was an old lady who lived nearby. The procedure at Mrs. Smith's was to knock and walk in. I would ask if she wanted owt from the shops. She always said she didn't, and added, "But thanks for callin." I'd be about to walk out the door then she would say, "Oh ah don't know, you couldn't call at so and so's could ya?" Then the rigmarole would begin a search for a pencil followed by a search for a bit of paper, it seemed to take ages. The list would invariably be longer than my mother's. By the time she had done ordering, then changing her mind, then changing her mind back again I didn't know if I was coming or going. When she finally handed me her note and money I'd shoot off before she decided to re-order something or other.

There was no money in it for me, because after one shopping expedition she gave me a penny. Taking my trousers off that night the penny fell out and my mother asked where I'd got it from, she went mad when I told her

Mrs. Smith had given it to me. I was warned, "Don't ever take anything off Mrs. Smith ever again." Not only that, but I was told to put my trousers back on and return my one penny reward.

On doing this Mrs. Smith said, "Oh you are a good boy Freddie." I answered, "Oh its O.K. Mrs. Smith." Just as I was about to leave the house Mrs. Smith called out, "Ya couldn't get me a fish frompt chip shop." Due to dialect, chip shop came out "Chip chop" but I knew what she meant.

I went to the "Chip chop"; there was a great big queue. Feeling mad I thought I'm like her personal slave. Also thinking I hope she's not sitting thinking of some other errand I could do when I get back. After what seemed an age I got to the front of the queue. I'd re-recorded my order in my head a thousand times. "Yes?" said the woman behind the counter I blurted out word perfect, "One fish with salt and vinegar wrapped to take out please." Only for the woman to say, "Fish'll be ten minutes, next please."

Chuffing ell I thought, 'fish n chip shop', but if you want fish you've got to wait, at this rate it'll take all night, an all because she gave me a penny for doing her shoppin. I made a vow never again would I accept a penny from old Mrs. Smith.

When I'd finally been served I dashed into Mrs. Smith's and plonked her fish on the table beside her. She said, "Oh you are a good lad." I felt as though she was nailing me to a cross with her next remark, "Ya can call any time Freddie." I got my hand on her door snek when she

74

called out to me, "Oh Freddie you didn't ask for salt n vinegar on me fish did ya?", adding, "Because I don't like salt and vinegar, it brings me out in spots." I answered in a flash, "No." On opening the door she called, "Tek this penny fu gooin." I thought, "Piss off," but answered, "Oh no it's all right Mrs. Smith." On shutting her door I heard the muffled sound of, "Yara good lad Freddie, Yara good lad."

My pal Dennis used to, at a very young age, have the job of reading the evening paper to her, on the excuse that her eyes were beginning to fail her. Dennis said he didn't mind doing her reading because more often than not she would drop off, when she did this he would make himself a cup of tea and sit in front of her fire reading the paper to himself. When he had finished his chore he would wake her up with a nudge. She would give him a penny for his trouble and off he'd go.

When I told Dennis my tale of taking the penny back he said, "Serves thi reight I spent my penny before I get back int house."

Anyway this particular day I called at Mrs. Smith's knocked and tried the door only to find it locked. The downstairs curtains were drawn I stepped back looked up at the bedroom window they were also closed. I made no more of it, dashed off towards the shops feeling good about the fact that I didn't have to do Mrs. Smith's shopping as well as me mam's.

On getting back home my mother remarked, "You've been quick," adding, "Did you go to Mrs. Smith's?" "Ah did but she must still be in bed, doors locked and curtains are shut." "At this time, somatts up, come on." Off we went to Mrs. Smith's. What with my mother bangin on the door and shoutin out her name, a small group of neighbours soon gathered outside her house.

A bloke propped a ladder up against Mrs. Smith's and began climbing it, with the intention of opening her bedroom window, only to be interrupted by another neighbours comments of, "that waistin thi time, I nailed winda's darn for her the other week." Someone commented, "Argh wi gonna gerin?"

I responded by saying, "Easy go downt' cellar grate, up cellar steps that way ya could open back door from inside." Someone chimed up "Good idea young un, go on then." There was an immediate silence and everyone looked at me. "What?" was my response. All the neighbours were unanimous it had to be me, being the only person small enough to fit down Mrs. Smith's cellar grate.

Encouraged by my mother's, "Go on it'll only take ya a minute." I squeezed down into the total blackness of Mrs. Smith's cellar. After a minute or two my eyes became accustomed to the darkness, and I could see the location of the cellar door due to a chink of light at the bottom of the door. Due to my apprehension I was up the cellar steps in a flash, I entered her living room and dashed to her downstairs window opened the curtains to let some light in. I approached her back door only to discover there was no key in it.

I looked at the window to see a load of faces peering in and calling out in muffled instructions, "C'mon open door," "Ah can't," I responded "Thiz no key int door." Then a woman that knew Mrs. Smith well advised "She keeps key fot door under her pillow every night." This remark scared me to death for while people were contemplating how to get into her house I heard comments like, "Ah bet shiz shook a six," (died), and "She looked ready fot Union Jack last time I saw her," (looked ready to die).

"She might be deerd," I argued. Some bloke outside remarked "Shill not hurt thi if she is." This comment brought a bout of laughter from the group of onlookers outside. But his observation scared the life out of me. My mother's face pushed to the front of the crowd outside to offer encouragement, "Go on Freddie it'll only take ya a tick." I approached Mrs. Smith's bedroom stairs with a great gulp to push down the lump in my throat; it did no good, because another lump took its place.

There was no carpet on the stairs, as I took my first step the stairs called out "creak" followed by my mournful call, "OYA THERE MRS. SMITH?" the same "creak" and call was repeated as I ascended, subconsciously counting each step. My mind stopped counting as I reached the one but last step twelve. This only added to my fear for I knew what number followed twelve.

The bedroom door was slightly ajar; I reached out and pushed the door ever so gently. It slowly drifted open with a sort of, "Weeeow." Mrs. Smith was laid flat on her back. My hair stood on end when I saw what was on the set

77

of drawers by her bedside. Her false teeth were in a thick glass of water. Due to the thickness of the glass they were magnified they looked huge and even more sinister they appeared to be laughing. I daftly thought they were probably laughing due to the fact they were no longer in Mrs. Smith's mouth.

As I approached her bed my heart was pounding, not in my body but in my head. "BADOOM, BADOOM, BADOOM." "OYA THERE MRS. SMITH?" I repeated again as I crept to the side of her bed. She lay motionless, eyes closed as white as a ghost, which seemed most apt, considering the conclusion I'd come to, that she was dead. I knelt down, "BADOOM, BADOOM, BADOOM." I gulped to get rid of the ever repeating lump in my throat. I shut my eyes, and plunged my hand under her pillow; I felt the movement of her head flop away to face the window.

I grasped the huge key pulling hard, on pulling the key hard, my hand and the keys momentum caused her head to flop over facing me. No more than inches from my face. "BADOOM, BADOOM, BADOOM." I was up on my feet and dashed for the bedroom door. Then horror of all horrors, I heard a call, "Is that you Freddie?" I spun round to see Mrs. Smith sat straight up in bed her eyes sticking out like chapel hat pegs, her white hair sticking out in all directions.

Christ she looked worse alive than when I thought she was dead, I screamed out, "ARRRRAGH," clutching the key I dashed down the stairs, in my haste I missed the last three steps and spilled into the downstairs room like the jackpot out of a fruit machine.

Despite this I kept up my running momentum by still running whilst on my knees. I plunged the key in the door, unlocked it, and opened the door. I pushed through the crowd of people entering, turning a deaf ear to all the enquiries, "Iz shi deerd?" "What's up?" "What's took ya so long?" I was up the entry and on to Martin Street in a flash, my heart still beating, "BADOOM, BADOOM, BADOOM."

A couple of months after this incident, word went round that once again nobody had seen Mrs. Smith for a while. On hearing this I scarped up to the tip with Dennis. No way was I going to repeat what had happened earlier in the year.

Sadly this time the worst had happened Mrs. Smith had sadly passed away. A week or so later her funeral had been organised. Dennis told me Mrs. Smith was laid out in her downstairs room in her coffin. Out of curiosity we dashed round to her house. The curtains of the house windows were shut as was the custom. Standing on her step was a funereal bloke dressed in black wearing a black top hat. He stood with his hands behind his back, on seeing us he said, "What are your two up to?" "Nowt," we replied, shaking our heads at the same time. Dennis blurted out pointing at me, "He used to do her shopping." "Oh," said the funeral bloke, "Would ya like to have a last look at her before we screw down the lid?" Straight away I thought not chuffing likely, if I'd have gone in she would have probably sat up and said something like, "Ooh Freddie you are getting a big lad." On making the offer he had a wry smile on his face knowing full well we would not take up the offer.

We peered past him to witness an eerie situation, an open coffin on the table. Due to the curtains being closed a pitch black room lit only by four flickering candles only added to the morbidity of the occasion. The bloke on the door called into the darkness to a couple of his associates, "O.K. lads get the lid on." They placed the lid on and began the gruesome task of screwing the lid down, an insidious sound if ever there was one. It was one that I would never forget. Creek, creek, squeak, squeak. After completing the task, one thing was for sure, Mrs. Smith had no chance of changing her mind. Two other funeral men entered the house, and the four blokes, one at each corner carried out the coffin, following the bloke on the door.

Half of Martin Street was out; the men on the street took their caps off their heads, while the women stood in little bunches holding their handkerchiefs to their mouths. As the hearse pulled away I felt a sort of guilty relief, due to the fact that I would no longer have to do her shopping ever again.

Mrs. Smith's house was soon allocated to new tenants, a family of four, man wife, and two lasses. They had only been in about a week when there was a knock on our door. It was the new tenant, the wife. My mother greeted her, "Hello love, settling in alright?" to which the woman answered, "We would be if it weren't fo your lad Fred." "Why what's up?" me mother questioned. "He keeps telling my kids house is haunted, and I can't get 'em to go to bed." My mother closed the door on her by saying, "Leave it we me love al soon sort it owt."

She then confronted me, "Did ya hear that? Thiv orny been ont street five minutes, an that at it benargh, if I hear any moor abarght that lot, al tec thi tut dog's ooerm oh tha listnin?" I answered with a deep sigh whilst staring at the fire.

Chapter 9

Straight from the horses!

Dennis and I were wondering down Martin Street one day and we bumped into a pal of mine Mick Daykin. Mick was a bit similar to us, always thinking things up to ease the boredom of the times.

Mick who was a year older than me said, "Hy ya Passey am glad ave bumped into ya." Mick had in his hand a box of drawing pins. "Were just one item short of havin a right laugh," declared Mick, "Horse muck." "Why horse muck?" I questioned. "Al tell ya soon," said Mick. Dennis quickly dived in, "It's all ort place." "Ah but it's got to be fresh horse muck," answered Mick.

I went on to say it wouldn't be a problem, because Mr. White the fruit man was a regular up and down Martin Street selling his fruit and veg direct from his horse drawn cart. The three of us sat on a wall waiting for Mr. White to appear, sure enough after about fifteen minutes we heard Mr. White calling out, "Get ya fruit and veg." We followed the call to the bottom of Burlington Street. Mr. White and his son Graham were selling their wares straight off the back of the cart.

We dashed towards them and looked on the floor at the back end of the horse, no luck. "What can ah do fo ya lads?" said Mr. White with a quizzical expression. "Nowt," I replied. We had no option but to follow Mr. White on his round.

Age 8 with cousin Marlene
out and about in Blackpool 1950

Uncle Ern

Age 9 marooned on a desert island with Marlene Blackpool 1951

Age 14 with Tony on our way to the fun fair
at Granville Road (Farm grounds)

After what seemed an age, Mr. White's horse cocked its tail up and produced the goods. It was steaming hot, to which Mick observed, "Perfect." Quick as a flash he pulled out of his pocket a brown paper bag, and equally as quick all three of us were filling it with steaming horse muck. Dennis remarked, "Ah hope it's gonna be weth it." "It will be," countered Mick. "What the bloody hell ya up to?" shouted Mr. White. The three of us ran off not bothering to reply.

Once we were a safe distance away from Mr. White, Mick explained his ruse. "Iz thi anybody ya want to get ya own back on?" We'd got a list as long as your arm, plus a few Mick had got in mind. Mrs. 'Miserable Get' for one, who by the way was now nicknamed Mrs. 'Shitpot', 'Filleted Phyllis' the chip shop scrooge, and many more.

Mick looked skywards, "Perfect," he said. We dived behind a wall at the sound of my mother's voice, she was at the top of our entry shouting into space, "Fred, come and get ya tea." The Fred bit was a bit elongated which made her call a call of importance, also a sign she was beginning to lose her temper. The three of us remained haggled up behind the wall out of sight. After three or four calls my mother grumbled something under her breath, and then disappeared down our entry.

Then Mick let us into the secret of his scam. Most of the doors around and on Martin Street did not have door knobs or latches, to enter the house; you held the handle of the door then pressed your thumb down on the latch which lifted the small arm of the latch upwards allowing you to enter.

It was by now dark. Mick got a bit of horse muck and flattened it between finger and thumb to the size of about the head of the drawing pin. Then put it on the spike of the drawing pin. Because the horse muck was still relatively fresh, it was still possible to flatten and mould. "What's gonna happen?" I was still puzzled. "Yul see, yul see," said Mick. "Pick somebody," "Mrs. 'Shitpot,'" said Dennis. "OK," said Mick, "Come on."

We got to Mrs. 'Shitpot's' house and ever so carefully Mick placed his drawing pin booby trap on the thumb part of Mrs. 'Shitpot's' latch. Because of the malleability of the horse muck, it was almost like plasticine, the horse muck, plus pin pointing upwards, stuck perfectly. Once in place, we as it says on boxes of fireworks, retreated to a safe distance. We hid behind a wall opposite.

After only a few minutes up the street walks Mr. 'Shitpot', he was obviously coming home from work. Although by his expression you could not tell, for like his wife he had the perfect face for a funeral director. "Watch," said Mick as he approached the door. Down his thumb went on the latch. "Ouch," he said, then better still, instinctively put his thumb in his mouth and sucked on it. "Erre, what the bloody ell?" Then started spitting. His wife came out, "What's up?" "Ah don't know," said Mr. 'Shitpot', "Somatts just stuck in mi thumb n ave gorra orrible taste in mi mouth." He looked at his thumb looked around, then disappeared in to the house.

It was perfect, the momentum of him pressing

down on the latch caused the pin and horse muck to stick to his finger, the sudden pulling away in shock of the pin sticking to his thumb, released the pin from his thumb. When he inspected his thumb there was no sign of horse muck, because he had already sucked his thumb clean. It was a perfect caper thanks to Mick.

We carried on for ages; we kept hearing our mothers calling for us, but it was no contest, and we were having a smashing time. We completed the trick on about a dozen or more victims, and each one had instinctively sucked on their thumb, and in most cases we retrieved the drawing pin to use again another day.

I knew I would be in trouble, but gave it no thought on getting back in the house.

> My Mother: "Wiv ya bin?"
> Me: "Just playing."
> Mother: "Didn't ya hear me shouting ya?"
> Me: "No, ave ya been shouting me?"
> Mother: "Ave been shouting ya till am blue int face."
> Me: (Trying to wriggle out of the question and answer sequence) "Do ya want owt fetching from't shops?"
> Mother: "Do ah want owt from shops? What ya been up to?"
> Me: "Just playin tiggy."
> Mother: "More like up to no good me lad, ya don't know ya born today, at one time at day I'd gerra

good hiding coming in late fo me tea."

She went on and on, I switched down the volume on my listening I was sitting staring at the fire. My mother awoke me by shouting "Are ya listening?"

Me: "Course I am."

Mother: "Well ya get ya tea, then its up them stairs to bed, thil be no listenin tut wireless fo you mi lad."

Another way of passing the time would be a visit to the pictures. It would usually be the 'Oxford', or the 'Western' on St. Phillip's Road, during holiday times it would sometimes be the 'Don' on 'Shalesmoor'. If ever we went to the 'Don' we would take packing up. For the film at the 'Don' would run continuously starting in the afternoon. The same programme was shown three or four times a day. So you could stop in and see the same programme twice or more for the same money, hence the packing up. Many's the time Dennis, Pete and I would be off to the 'Don' with packing up of bread and dripping and a bottle of water.

Sometimes we'd get in towards the end of the main feature, so in effect watched the film backwards. We'd watch the end first, stay in and watch the beginning after. It didn't really matter what the film was, it was better than looking at the wireless. The films around that time were usually feel good films and an escape from the dour conditions of the day. As a little lad of about nine years old I used to like Rhonda Fleming, I secretly thought she was beautiful. We got in the 'Don' one day to see the ending of a film starring Rhonda Fleming and John Payne. They were just telling this little kid of about my age, that they were adopting him. The little kid was a cripple with irons on each leg, no doubt to add some sentiment to the film. Well they tell this little kid he's part of the family, then John Payne announces, "We've brought you a present," and brings out this lovely fawn coloured Shetland pony. No doubt it was stupefying in its corniness, but we watched the end, then the beginning, then from beginning to end. I couldn't help thinking, "Ah wish owd Rhonda would adopt me."

After about four hours of pictures at the 'Don', we would trapse back to Martin Street with our bottle of water. By now it had about two inches of water in the bottom with lumps of bread and dripping swimming around in it.

School in those days was strict and regimental. If you learned anything it was probably in spite of the teachers and not because of them, march to and from class single file, and repeat the times tables parrot fashion every day.

During one particular class, one of the lad's mothers came into the classroom and, after giving our teacher some sheet music, left. Her lad was one of the very few, better dressed variety of pupil. Always smartly dressed and always wore a tie. Norman was his name, Norman was, at the time, a fat little lad, and due to the fact he came from a more wealthy family than most of us, was never picked on by the teacher. The teacher seemed to like Norman. On the downside, anyone liked by the teacher was disliked, through no fault of his own, by most of the other kids. I felt sorry for Norman in a strange way.

After concluding the lesson our teacher announces that we are going into the hall for a music lesson. He hit his cane down once, we all stood, he hit his cane down again, we all shuffled into single lines, brought his cane down again and we all filed out from the left into a single line. When we got into the hall we all had to sit in a semi-circle crossed legged on the floor. I hated it because the floor was made up of sort of wooden bricks, if you shuffled about you would invariably get a splinter up your arse.

The music teacher was a fussy woman who we nicknamed Mrs. 'Flabbergasted' for obvious reasons. She was at the piano; our teacher would act as a sort of conductor, the pain inflicting type. He gave Mrs. 'Flabbergasted' the sheet music that Norman's mother had given him. He then announced that we were in for a treat, he went on about Norman having singing lessons and that he was going to entertain us by singing a couple of songs. Norman looked as surprised as the rest of us at the announcement. The teacher called Norman to the front. Norman's face was like a big red tomato, he was embarrassed to death at the prospect of singing to us.

We all sat wondering what he was going to sing. We didn't have to wait long, the teacher announced Norman was going to sing 'Daddy wouldn't buy me a bow wow' to which somebody declared, "Chuffin ell." The teacher went berserk and demanded total silence. Then tapping his cane said, "One, two, three", and away Mrs. 'Flabbergasted' 'went' on her piano. Norman, by this time, was looking as though he could burst, and started singing his 'Daddy wouldn't buy me a bow wow'.

I don't know how much his mother paid for his singing lessons but it was a waste of money. There was more melody in a ragman's call. Having completed his song, the teacher declared, "Wonderful," and we were all ordered to applaud. Norman looked visibly relieved having completed his song. All of a sudden it got worse for him. The teacher announced, "Now Norman's going to sing, wait for it, 'If I could plant a tiny seed in the temple of your heart'."

The piano started up, and then just as he was about to sing somebody made a raspberry noise. The teacher waved his cane to signal to stop the song, then demanded in a strict authoritative tone, "Who trumped?" It was the day after the horse muck caper, I never thought there would be repercussions but there were. "Will the trumper own up?" said the teacher, by this time everyone was rolling about getting splinters up there arse, but still laughing. Tears were rolling down my cheeks, but not for long.

While performing the horse muck caper I had each time wiped the stained palms of my hands on the back of my trousers. On leaving the house that morning my mother had said, "Yu smell funny this mornin." I never gave it another thought and dashed off to school. I had a bit of a scuffle with a lad in the playground before school because he said to me, "Passey tha smells like a pile o shit."

So back to the music lesson, having not got a volunteer for his, "Who's trumped?" The teacher said he would, "Smell out the culprit." He went around smelling at each individual kid. Got to me, sniffed put two and two together made five and gave me the cane for trumping in class. Even farting was outlawed in school in those days. I couldn't plead my innocence and tell the teacher about our horse muck caper I just had to wince and bear it. Norman completed his singing.

For a long time I could not walk past a pile of horse muck without picking up a choice warm piece for use in any opportunity that might crop up. I always had two or three drawing pins in the top pocket of my coat for the same reason.

One day such an opportunity arose. We were all lined up ready after assembly to march into our class. Our teacher Mr. 'Cloutem' would always walk in front of the queue put his thumb on the snek door of our classroom, push the door open, then order, "Right in you go," with an added order, "An no talking." On this particular morning as he was about to open the door he was overcome with a bout of sneezing, during the sneezing his eyes began to run. He took off his glasses to wipe his eyes, he placed his glasses on a window sill, his glasses were of the bottle bottom variety, and he was completely blind without them. Quick as a flash one of the kids in front of me picked up the teachers glasses and put them in his pocket.

After groping around for his glasses, Mr.

'Cloutem' began to panic due to the fact he could not find them. With his eyes squinting he called out, "Boys someone pass me my glasses." When no one did he grabbed a kid by the shoulder and ordered, "Go fetch a teacher." The lad dashed off, the teacher, still blinded, shouted out "Keep still and no talking." It was a golden chance I could not miss. I tip toed to the front of the queue and set up my booby trap. The kid who had inadvertently helped me set up the scam, returned the glasses to where he had picked them up. One or two of the kids started giggling to which the blind teacher called out, "Quiet or I'll cane the lot of you."

The youngster who had gone for help came back with, of all people, the headmaster who enquired, "Now what seems to be the trouble?" Our teacher replied, "I put my glasses on the window sill sir, and I can't see to find them." The head retorted with a brusque sort of manner, "Well here you are, they are just where you left them!" Our teacher answered, "Oh thank you sir."

Then once composed he leaned over putting his thumb flush on our classroom snek. "Ouch," he jumped at the shock, and then it was mission completed when he shoved the afflicted thumb straight into his mouth. "Ergh." He spat out making all sorts of noises.

Once he had recovered he inspected the door snek and in a slightly puzzled tone he ordered, "Every one in class." It proved to be my final escapade for on getting home my mother sniffed around me and said, "You smell like a pile of shit. Tek them cloths off, its bath fo you m'lad then its up them stairs to bed."

Chapter 10

A new residence, a new school

The year is 1952; we have left our one-up-one-down house in Martin Street, Upperthorpe. Thanks to dad working at the Hallamshire Steel & File we acquired a firm's house at 19, Boyland Place, Neepsend. Compared to our previous dwelling in Martin Street, our terrace house on Boyland Place was a veritable palace. For this was not a one-up-one-down back-to-back house. Oh no! It was a two-up-two-down with living room plus kitchen and more importantly two bedrooms.

For the first time in our lives, Brian and I would have our very own bedroom. For Brian, who was seventeen at the time, and me aged ten, things were definately looking up. Boyland Place ran off Boyland Street, which itself ran off Neepsend Lane. Boyland Place by incorporating Manor Street formed a boomerang shape with terrace type houses facing each other.

Another added bonus was that we would have our very own outside toilet. On the downside Boyland Street, Boyland Place, and Manor Street were bang smack in the middle of an industrial district of Sheffield. In fact the back drop of our yard in Boyland Place was the bar straightening mill of the Hallamshire, Stones Brewery ran all along one side of Boyland Street, and a railway line ran along the back of the houses on Manor Street.

When my dad had heard there was a possibility of

him getting this house, I had gone along with my mam and dad to have a sneak look. I had commented that, "It seemed to be foggy." "Ho no!" my dad had retorted, "Its not fog, its smoke frompt firm."

I at the age of ten was a bit apprehensive at the thought of leaving Martin Street, not the housing conditions or the school but because I'd be leaving my pals behind, Pete, Lawrence and Dennis. I need not have worried for over the wall from us lived the Higgins family man, wife and about six kids.

On our first day in the house I looked over our wall to see a football match in progress. On seeing me, Chick Higgins, who was a couple of years older than me, smiled. He then said the magical words, "Wanna game?" I was over the wall in a flash and was integrated into the area in no time.

Sleeping in our new dwelling was difficult at first due to the fact that the bar straightening mill, close to our backyard, was in operation twentyfour hours a day five days a week.

Stones' brewery lorries would form a queue starting at 7am, up Boyland Place and all along Manor Street. In turn they would enter the brewery for loading up. So what with the noise in our backyard, the brewery lorries constantly being started up, the smoke from the Hallamshire, petrol fumes and then chuck in the odd screaming express hurtling along the back of Manor Street, it was hardly an English country garden type of set up. Sometimes on walking outside you could feel solid little particles landing on you, something like snowdrops, but it was not snow; it was solidifying muck which contained goodness knows what. But my dad and mam were smiling on the upgrade in housing conditions so we all felt generally better off.

Woodside School stood on the right hand side of the steep Rutland Road. As of the times it was much like my former school Crookesmoor. A Victorian miserable, imposing sort of building which seemed to shout out 'house of correction' not place of learning. One extra bonus from leaving Crookesmoor School was that I was leaving my teacher, the one I'd nicknamed Mr. 'Cloutem'.

On my first day I felt pretty good, I should have known better for my new teacher was much the same as old Mr. 'Cloutem'. I had described Mr. 'Cloutem' as having a face like a well kept grave. Well my new teacher had a face about as welcoming as the cemetery gates, and within no time at all I would be referring to him as Mr. 'Pain'. He was about six feet tall, wore glasses, and also wore a permanently miserable expression. As with my previous teacher, he was smartly turned out in three piece suit and tie and as for his build was not much thicker than the stick he used to wield.

I often wondered as a kid, were these canes standard issue for teachers? I could picture in my imagination some bloke saying to prospective teachers, "Right you've passed, here's a box of chalks, a pen, and a propelling pencil, and don't forget your cane." If they were standard issue, who bought them, and where from, also did they have cane exhibitions at Earls Court where potential buyers could view the latest in pain inflicting sticks. If this was so, what happened to the cane manufacturers?

Well Mr. 'Pain's' favourite subject was Religious Education. He used to go to great lengths to explain the virtues of Jesus and God, in between hitting you with the cane. He was a sort of eye for an eye bloke, definitely not a turn the other cheek chappie.

One day he warned us that we would have a double helping of R.E. He also said he would be asking for our observations on this double lesson. His double lesson consisted of him reading The Bible to us, which to a ten year old didn't make much sense at all. I for one didn't mind, for while I sat supposedly listening, my mind would be off thinking about 'Wednesday's' next match at Hillsborough or what was on at the 'Roscoe' pictures, in fact all sorts of things.

Anyway, after this double lesson he demanded, "Observations please." No one volunteered to put their hand up. "What have you learned from my readings?" There was no reaction. To my horror he said, "You Pass, stand up." Filled with trepidation I did so, "What have you learned?" he demanded. Not knowing what to say, I said the first thing that came into my head, "He wer a good bloke that Jesus." Mr. 'Pain' smashed his cane on his desk to stifle the giggles of the class and ordered me to the front. "Hold your hand out lad," you've not been paying attention, and promptly smashed the cane down on my outstretched hand.

On sitting down he repeated, "Observations, I demand your observations." To all the class's surprise a hand shot up, it was a lad called Walter Osgathorpe. "That's better," said the teacher, "Stand up Walter and give us your conclusions." Walter said, "Well sir," then he hesitated, "Yes Osgathorpe, go on boy, go on." Walter then said, "Try to do everythin reight, and thal end up nailed to a cross." It was said in all innocence and had the class laughing. How did Mr. 'Pain' react? He proved Walter's observations to be correct, by giving him the cane. I never knew the teacher's first name but 'Puritanical' would have suited him, yes, 'Puritanical Pain'.

Down the back of Woodside School ran Woodside Lane. Jim Thorpe, the local bookmaker, lived in Woodside Lane, and betting being illegal at the time, 'putting a bet on' was a bit of a cloak and dagger operation. Jim had 'runners' all over Sheffield. A 'bookies runner' would be a bloke who collected bets from the public and handed over the bets and money to Jim the bookmaker. He generally worked on a commission basis. Well as my dad and mam liked a bet, after going home for my dinner, my mother would say, "Put us a bet on, on your way back to school." The bets would vary, an example would be three tanner doubles, and a tanner treble, two bob in all. (A tanner being six old pennies - 2½p, and two bob being two shillings - 10p,).

Jim Thorpe lived on the right hand side of Woodside Lane. Facing his house, a bit further up the lane, would stand one of his 'runners'. He would stand in-between a gap in the houses, and at the end of the gap was the outer wall of Woodside School. This 'runner' was a spiv like character who would stand in the shadows out of sight of any inquisitive Bobby. Any sign of the police and word would soon be conveyed to the 'runner' and he would be off.

The 'runner' on Woodside Lane was dressed in a large Gabardine Mac, with a Trilby perched on the back of his head and a cig permanently in his mouth. Inside the Mac were two specially made deep pockets, one for money, and the other one was for the bets.

Word soon got round Boyland Place that I was going to the 'bookies runner' on my way back to school, so in no time I was collecting bets from all sorts of people to put on for them. Each bet would have a pseudonym at the bottom. Then if you had any winnings to come you would go to Jim Thorpe's house tell him your pseudonym, and he would pay you out.

My dad's pseudonym was 'Joe 20'. The name in the pseudonym you used was usually followed by a number to avoid the confusion of anyone using the same pseudonym. Also if you got caught with incriminating evidence of the bets the police would be no wiser on who was placing the bet. People would give me a tanner for taking their bets, plus a tanner and sometimes a bob for fetching their winnings, depending on how lucky they were.

So at ten years old I could earn a pound a week from taking bets. One thing I did not look forward to was fetching the winnings. I would go up to Jim Thorpe's and knock on the door. If Jim answered it he would say, "Don't knock, just walk in. Chuffin coppers will notice if kids are forever knocking at the door. You'll get us all locked up." The next time I'd go I'd walk straight in and it wouldn't be Jim but his wife who'd go mad saying, "You cheeky little bleeder, haven't you got any manners?" Then she would send me back out telling me to knock first.

I always approached the house with trepidation. You could bet if I knocked it would be Jim who would give me a rollicking for knocking, if I didn't, it would be his wife who would give me a rollicking for walking straight in. Jim's house was like an Aladdin's Cave. The table and sideboard would have various glass bowls all full of money, one full of threepenny bits, one full of tanners, one for the bobs, one for the two bobs, and likewise for the half-crowns, also piles of ten bob notes, pound notes and fivers. Bookmaking was obviously a lucrative business.

When giving the 'runner' the bets and money I noticed he never counted them, he just shoved the bets in one deep pocket and the money in the other. This was usually followed by the words, "Get thee sen off kid," while nervously looking round. I would then walk past him, drop over the wall, and into school. The wall on his side was about two feet high, and on the school side it was about six feet high. I could slither down the wall and into the school.

The fact that the 'runner' did not count the money against the bets placed prayed on my mind. So much so I decided to have a bet myself. I thought I'd write a bet out and shove it with the other bets, but not add any money. So this dinnertime I'm having my dinner whilst looking at the Morning Telegraph, the racing page headline read, 'Vulgan's Pride in with a chance.'

Through taking bets I'd noticed most of the bets were of the accumulative type - doubles and trebles, I'd also learned that these bets very rarely paid off. I supposed people were gambling in small amounts and hoping for large returns. So while my mother wasn't looking I wrote out, ten bob win 'Vulgan's Pride' and my pseudonym was 'Dennis 2', as a sort of mark of respect to my old pal Dennis Aistrop.

I had my heart in my mouth as I approached the 'bookies runner', but sure enough the money went in one pocket and the bets in the other, and I was off over the wall and into school.

Later that night my dad was reading the Stop Press in The Star and declaring, "Waste o money, bleedin orses, down ageern." "Has Vulgan's Pride won?" I nervously asked. "Argh," he said, "four to one, bleedin headlines it wer an all int morning papers." My heart started pounding, ten bob at four to one is two quid, plus my ten bob which I'd not put on makes two pound ten shillings. "Am just off arght," I said, and I was off up Woodside Lane to collect my winnings. I knocked on the door and sure enough it was Jim Thorpe. "What av I told ya about knocking ont door just walk in." "Dennis 2," I blurted out. Jim looked through all these bits of paper then declared, "Two pounds ten", then he hands me two pound notes plus a ten bob note and I'm in heaven.

Next day I decide it's so easy I'll repeat my little caper, so I'm off after dinner up Woodside Lane with my bets in one hand that contained a ten bob win for myself and the money for the bets in the other not including the ten bob I've had on. I hand over the bets and money to the 'runner' and I'm just about to run off to school when the 'runner' grabs me by the scruff of my neck and says, "Wait there, I was ten bob down yesterday so lets have a look at ya bets."

He then declares, "Your ten bob short." I began to blush up to the roots and then I take the bets back off him and pull out my prospective ten bob win and say, "Oh, ah don't think Mrs. Smith gave me the money for that bet," and screwed the bet up chucking it on the floor. The 'bookies runner' grabbed my ear and gave it a great big twist saying, "If tha does that ageern al have thi guts fo garters, o tha listnin tha little twat?" I said, "Sorry mister", and I'm off in a flash and into school. I continued to take bets to him, but after that he always checked the money and the bets.

"Right schools over for the day," said Mr. 'Pain'. Then he scared the life out of me by saying, "Pass will you stay behind." My mind was in turmoil wondering what I'd done wrong. When I was alone with him he said, "I've noticed that when you return from dinner you slither down the wall opposite," pointing with his cane. He went on to ask, "Why don't you use the school gates." "Oh, I go to my pals sir," I dare n't tell him I'm putting bets on thinking he'd probably explode with all his puritanical thoughts.

"Don't lie to me boy," he shouts bringing the cane down sharply on his desk. "I have it on good authority that you place bets for people in the vicinity on a regular basis." He went on, "In fact I have observed you myself on numerous occasions, so don't dare deny it." I replied, "Ah just do it for neighbours as a favour," thinking he's got me bang to rights so lets get it over with. "You do realise that gambling is illegal?" "Yes sir."

"I want to ask you something Pass. What would you do if a policeman were to approach you while you were conducting your illegal activity?" "I'd scarpa sir," I reply. "Translate for me boy the word scarpa." "I'd do a runner," I translate. "And what would you do if you were caught by a policeman, would you then divulge all the names of the people who were placing bets?" "Oh no sir, because then I'd be in trouble with everybody."

Mr. 'Pain' went on, "So you provide this service for free?" Seeing that he was putting words into my mouth I decided to go along with him, "Yes sir." "I suppose in a diverse way you are being community minded?" said Mr. 'Pain'. "Oh yes sir," I confirmed, "Some people have bad legs and can't make it up to Woodside Lane." "Very well then Pass, we will hear no more about it then."

I couldn't believe my ears, this bloke who would readily cane you for sneezing, or coughing in class and who was fond of quotations from the bible was turning a blind eye to illegal activities. "Before you go Pass," he went on, "A mans word should be his bond, you agree?" I didn't know where this was leading but readily agreed, "Oh yes sir."

"So Pass I will let you into a little secret, one that you must never repeat. I have an on-going project into the whys and wherefores of gambling, and Pass you could help me. If I gave you a bet would you be willing to help me with my project by placing the wager?" "Yes sir," thinking wake me up I'm dreaming. "So as from tomorrow when I call for dinnertime see that you are last to leave the class and my project will be our secret."

So from then on I would be last out of class for dinner and he would have the bet written out with the money wrapped up inside it. Everyday he would have three tanner doubles and a tanner treble, two bob in all.

I used to keep any money I'd got in a jam jar under the bed. As for Mr. 'Pain's' bets, I never put them on. I chucked his money, along with his bets in my jam jar. I always checked if he had any winnings to come, and it only happened once, he won three bob and I paid him out from his own money from my jam jar.

The pseudonym he used was 'Moses 10'. From that day on we almost became friends. No matter what indiscretion I committed, he overlooked it, he never caned me again – easy street.

All his praying didn't help him pick any winners, but made me a few bob as his disciple.

Chapter 11

Exit Woodside

Having failed my eleven plus at Woodside Junior School, it was with some apprehension that I approached Burngreave Secondary. I was standing around chatting to a lad a year older than myself in the school yard. He began giving me the benefit of his one year experience, marking my card if you like. "It depends on whose class you get in," he said, then went on to give a catalogue of ill treatment by certain teachers.

While he was chatting a bloke rides into the playground on a motorbike, immediately a big cheer goes up and the man on the motorbike gives a sort of royal wave to all the kids. He was small, good looking, probably in his early thirties, wearing a duffle coat and a university type scarf that trailed in the wind as he rode in. "Oh that's Taffy," declared my informant, "Ya get in his class and thas cracked it. He's a right laugh never canes anybody."

The lad went on to tell me the procedure of the playground. "A teacher gives a blast on the whistle, at which you must freeze on the spot, don't move," he went on, "Or yull get cane." Then he said, "He will blow his whistle again and each class has to form a single line. On the third blast of the whistle each line then marches off to their respective classes."

Sure enough out comes this teacher who turned

out to be appropriately nicknamed 'Stoneface'. His first blast rendered a throbbing mass of chattering kids motionless. You could hear a pin drop. A breeze was getting up, and due to the immediate silence sounded like a gale. The whistleblower did not immediately give a second blast, but surveyed his motionless audience by slowly moving his head from right to left. All of a sudden he shouted, "Palmer by my side at once." This lad of about thirteen dashes from somewhere behind me and stands by his side. He looks around very slowly and again barks, "Wilson by me side."

At the second whistle he announces, "Line up, new boys in front of me," he indicates by holding the palm of his hand to his chest. He gives his whistle a second blast and as if by magic, or by some invisible magnet, there are about a dozen orderly lines of kids. I being one of the new kids am about third from the front of a line of forty kids or so.

The winds getting up and my hair blows down across my forehead. "YOU BOY," old 'Stoneface' shouts, with his face no more than six inches from mine, "BY MY SIDE." He gives his whistle another blast and off everyone troops to their respective class. While the three of us shuffle along behind 'Stoneface'.

The kid on my right whispers, "Don't pick thinnest," I whisper back, "What ya on a barght?" He just repeats, "Don't pick thinnest," in an even lower whisper. Anyway in we troop to this blokes ground floor school room, all his class are totally silent. On the wall is a sort of canvass bag, rolled up, and held by two strings, he pulls at two of the strings and down rolls the bag to expose half a dozen canes of various thicknesses. All of a sudden, "Don't pick thinnest," made sense.

"Palmer," he bellows, "Which one?" Palmer replies, "The second one down sir." He draws out the cane demands, "Hold out your hand," then promptly smashes it down on the lad's hand. Palmer grimaces, screws his pain inflicted hand up and shuffles off. "Wilson," commands the teacher, 'Whispering Wilson' then says, "Third one down sir," the teacher repeats the punishment to Wilson and off he goes, holding his damaged hand under his armpit.

While these two punishments are inflicted my heart's pounding in my head and I'm feeling scared to death, not at the prospect of getting the cane, but by the clinical way the punishment was metered out. "Ah," the teacher says looking directly at me, "New boy eh? What's your name?" "Pass," I reply. "Is that your name, or some sort of declaration that you don't know your name?" His class giggles at his comments; surprisingly he does not correct them, and probably basking in the glory of his joke attempted comment.

"Which one then Pass?" he says. He was still holding cane number three in his hand, and as 'Whispering Wilson' seemed to know the score, I reply, "Number three sir," he then demands, "Hold out your hand." With my brain being occupied in making a logical choice of cane without thinking I held out my right hand; a terrible mistake, because being right handed it meant my punishment would carry the extra burden of doing school work with a damaged hand. I'd no time to change my mind, down smashed the cane; he proceeded the action with the words, "Welcome to Burngreave School Pass." He then directed me to my new classroom, "Out of this door, turn right, up the stairs first classroom on your right."

As I walked up the steps to my new classroom I was thinking "What a start," I had had the cane before schoolwork had officially started. I sheepishly entered the classroom and I saw my new teacher. At the first sight of him my hopes were immediately uplifted. Yes it was Taffy, the no caning laugh a minute most popular teacher in the school. I thought, as my informant told me, "Cracked it."

I gingerly entered the classroom; Taffy looked up from his desk and asked, "Where have you been?" He then declared, "Oh 'Stoneface' has had you hasn't he?" He then went on to amaze me by saying, "He's a twat of a bloke, and he really is." He checked his register and said "You're Pass then?" I nodded in reply, "Lets look at your hand," he said, "Are you right handed?" "Yes sir." "Big mistake, always offer your non writing hand. Go to the toilet, first left then right, let the tap run and hold your hand under it whilst wriggling your fingers, you'll soon have the circulation back. If you get stopped, tell who ever, you have my permission to go to the toilet. If you get seen in the toilet with your hand under the tap, you're washing your hands, right?" "Yes sir" and then I'm off to the toilet.

As I pass the head teachers door it suddenly opens and the head shouts, "You boy stop. Where are you going?"

"To the toilet sir." "Have you got permission?" "Yes sir."
"Very well on your way." Despite wearing my very first pair
of long trousers I felt very young and vulnerable in this big
school with big kids. In the school at Woodside I felt like a
piranha in a pond of goldfish, and somehow now I felt I'd
turned into a chuffin goldfish.

I returned to the class after the cold water
therapy feeling much better. I felt even better when
Taffy said, "Pass, you're excused all writing duties for
today just listen and learn. Lesson one, go along with
'Stoneface's' game, if you can't, or won't, don't ever
offer him your writing hand."

The first lesson was history, but Taffy said, "We'll
not bother with that today, I'll tell you about my exploits
in the R.A.F. as a Spitfire pilot." He went on for about forty
minutes keeping us all amused and amazed at his devil may
care attitude during the war. This teacher was too good to
be true.

Chapter 12

Gulp

The fact that I began my education at Burngreave in Taffy's class meant my initial trepidation of starting a new school for bigger boys was replaced by optimism. There wasn't a day went by that did not include laughs or wartime stories. His manner produced a relaxed atmosphere that was totally alien to the rest of this highly strict and regimented establishment. My previous two schools, Crookesmoor and Woodside Junior Schools were grimy, imposing Victorian buildings, which I suppose were a reflection of the times. Like the other two, Burngreave School was built on a hill, but it was brick built and a more modern looking school. I suppose staff attitude was very similar to that of my previous two schools, but not in Taffy's class.

Railings separated the boys from the girls, and one day Taffy, whilst reminiscing on his war time heroics, wistfully looked across to the girl's side. He interrupted his commentary by saying, "The girls are having some sort of gym class, mmm if you get a chance lads, at playtime have a gander at Doreen Nuttall. Oh what a smasher."

On the Thursday of the first week Taffy announced that we should bring our football or rugby gear the following day, for Friday's last two lessons were sports times. We would all troupe off to sports fields on

Stubbin Lane. I could not wait to get involved in football. I was slightly disappointed the next day when Taffy told us that the teacher who was to take us for football was ill, and that he would take us for his favourite sport, 'rugger' as he called it.

Well it was Friday and it was better than sitting in the classroom, so I thought I'd make the best of it. Up on Stubbin Lane Taffy split up the class to about twenty a side, produced a rugby ball and asked, "Any questions?" I approached him and said, "I don't know owt about rugby sir." So he gave me the basic run down, "When you pass the ball you must pass it backwards, if you kick it, kick it forwards, and the object of the game," he said, "Was to get this," pointing to the ball, "Over the oppositions line." "Off you go," he said after blowing his whistle.

I had noticed all the players congregating in the middle of the field, so I stayed out wide in space, and tried to keep myself behind play and ready to run with the ball towards the opposition's line. Sure enough the ball was thrown to me. I was a fairly strong runner and off I went. As most of the kids were disinterested it was easy to do so. I kept repeating this over and over again, spurred on by Taffy's encouraging cries of, "Bravo."

At half time he said, "I've devised a plan to stop you, let's see how you handle it." This time when I received the ball I was faced by two or three lads, so I kicked the ball forward, then ran past them to score again. As an eleven year old I got no satisfaction at all, and rugby, due to my ignorance of the sport, seemed daft. I even felt daft playing it. "Well done Pass," said Taffy and off home I went dreaming of next Friday, when I could revert to football.

The following Thursday when the class broke up at the end of school Taffy asked me to hang back. "Pass," he said, "Tomorrow when the teacher that takes you for football asks who's for football, you keep your hand down; 'rugger's' the game for you." I was horrified at the thought and retorted, "I don't even like rugby sir." "You will learn to Pass," Taffy retorted. "No I won't," I said. "And I'm telling you, you will, so get yourself off and don't forget keep your hand down tomorrow," said Taffy.

I went home a bit down in the mouth, all I ever wanted to do was play football, and anyway the only reason I'd done alright at rugby was because out of about forty kids only about half a dozen had tried at all. I thought, in my ignorance, rugby had been invented for kids who couldn't play football.

The time came round the following day when into our class burst this enthusiastic bloke who announces, "Right lads who's for football this afternoon?" Taffy's eyes were fixed on my face. I hesitated for a moment, should I defy Taffy the most popular teacher I'd ever known, or go with my first love of football. So I put my hand up. As I put my hand up Taffy's eyes looked down at the papers on his desk in front of him. The teacher jotted down everyone's name that would be playing football and off he went.

Taffy carried on with his teaching and never mentioned it again, so I thought well he's not that bothered. I did OK at football and scored a few goals. So the following Monday I was off to school full of life. During our first lesson, which was English, in comes the bloke who had taken us for football to announce team points acquired by the lads who had taken part in the football. The school ran a four house system and on one side of the teacher was a sort of league table in four different colours. The idea was to encourage a competitive edge, and build a team spirit. When he finally got to me he declared, "Pass ten team points well done," and off he went.

The English lesson that I was doing was composition, in other words writing stories. It was my favourite lesson except for football. After completion the books were gathered up by one pupil for each respective row, of four rows, and then placed on the teacher's desk for marking. Whilst he was busy marking, the class would be told to do a bit of reading.

After the work had been marked the books were then returned by the kids who had first collected them. I was puzzled to say the least that our teacher took only fifteen minutes to read and mark forty compositions or essays as they call them today. I opened my book and across the bottom were the words, 'Complete drivel, minus ten house points,' in red ink. He had begun his war of attrition.

Whatever the lesson he would invite comments from me then put me down with words, to the laughter of the class. This went on for a few months and my schoolwork was going down hill fast. We had a sort of dummy run for a forthcoming exam, I finished last. I hated school, my self esteem was non existent, and he poked fun at me to the class who were good lads. I could not blame them for laughing for if it had been anyone else I would probably have been laughing too.

In one English lesson the topic was, "What's in a name?" He went on to say, "If your name was Cooper you probably descended from barrel makers, Smith from a blacksmith etc." He then announced, "Mr. Pass come to the front, lets see what we can make of your name."

I was full of trepidation standing in front of the whole class knowing that I was about to be ridiculed; he was going to be the joker and I the stooge. When you are getting on twelve and in long trousers you think you are grown up, so I even felt ashamed of my own trepidation. "Ah Pass, what can we make of your name?" he said in a very loud voice, "As your work has been nothing short of backward these last few months, please take the chalk and write your name backwards on the blackboard please." I did so with trembling hands, "No such word," he said, "Rub out the first S." I did so leaving the word 'sap'. "Ah now we're getting some where, lets have a look at what the dictionary has to say, 'to undermine', yes that fits the bill also, 'a trench' which explains the heights you've hit with your learning at this school, and more revealing 'a juice of plants'," all this said to the amusement of the rest of the class, "Yes Pass sit down you are a bit of a plant aren't you?"

At playtime the inevitable happened, a kid in our

class began to poke fun at me calling me amongst other things 'plant'. I told him to, "Piss off," but he continued; only this time he began prodding me. Push came to shove and we rolled about in a sort of scrimmage, kids of eleven and twelve don't fight but roll about in a sort of well, scrimmage. We were soon surrounded by a circle of kids chanting, "A FEIGHT." "A FEIGHT." "A FEIGHT." Old 'Stone-face' burst through the ring of kids and pulled us apart. He was almost gleeful at the situation, and I could just picture myself picking the cane. All of a sudden up pops Taffy, "These are my boys," he says to 'Stone-face', "I'll handle this." He then says, "You two, to the classroom at once."

We were both standing in front of the class as all the other boys trooped in. When everyone was settled, Taffy points to me and says, "Look at the size of you compared to little Jimmy." As I was one of the biggest lads in the class I towered over Jimmy. "What we have here in front of you is a bully." I could not believe my ears. "I dint start it," I blurted out. "How dare you interrupt me?" Taffy said. He then told Jimmy to go to his seat while he went on about bullies and how cowardly they were. The word 'sap' was still on the blackboard in a corner. After berating me more, he ordered me to write 'bully' in front of 'sap', then said, "Get to your seat you're pathetic."

Oh how I missed my pals from Martin Street. Taffy being so popular with everyone was cutting me off from all the rest of the class; I felt that I was truly alienated. A few days later a similar incident happened and the whole routine was repeated.

I began dreading the thought of going to school. Friday night I'd be OK, for I would not be facing the prospect of going to school, but as Sunday wore on I began to become more and more immersed with worry. On Monday morning I would run to our outside toilet to be physically sick. This happened day after day, my mother said, "Whatever's the matter with you, is everything OK at school?" "Yes, corse it is," I'd reply. I felt that by telling my mother my problems I would be acting like a baby and me now in long trousers. Besides things were looking up on the home front, my mam and dad had now got a record player, and after seeing, at the age of six, my mother saying, "I wish I could die," I could not bring myself to tell her anything that would cause her to worry.

I devised a plan for dinnertime and playtime; I would keep a low profile by sitting in a corner of the schoolyard and watch the bigger lads play football. Two lads stood out I remember, one lad called Fantham who went on to play for Wednesday and England, and another called Fox. I was sitting there one day, when through the crowd of lads playing football came marching this lad; he was called 'Biffa' due to his size, and demeanour.

He never took his eyes off me. I never moved, what could he want me for? As I sat there he said, "I'm little Jimmy's brother," then clenched a fist, drew back his right arm underhand and smashed it into my left eye. I felt a sudden pain in my eye, then a sudden pain on the back of my head as my head went back and hit the wall behind, then someone switched the lights out. As the lights came back on I was helped to my feet by one of the teachers who was telling my teacher what had happened. "I'll sort it," said Taffy, "Both of you to my room."

'Biffa' and I stood before the class. I was looking through one eye, but thought well at least I can't be branded a bully as 'Biffa' towered above me and was built like a brick shit house. He was about fourteen and I was getting on twelve. Taffy entered the room and said to 'Biffa', "Get off to your class; I don't want to see you before me again." Once 'Biffa' had left Taffy pointed to my eye and then said, "This is what you get when you are a bully, I have no sympathy for you at all Pass, sit down."

I went home with this huge black eye and when my dad said, "What's tha been doin, feightin?" I replied, "Argh dad." My mother said, "Thiz sommat up at that school." My dad argued, "Don't be daft, kids o alust feightin. Thiz nowt up at school is thi Fred lad?" "No," I lied.

On the next street to us lived the Ferneoughs, a family with two lads Roy and Ernest. Ernest was a big friendly lad of about fourteen; from time to time I'd sit on our wall and listen to him playing Frankie Laine records. He would often shout, "Come on over ya can have job of putting records on for me." His record player played just one record at a time, so off I'd go, and I got to like putting records on for Ernie.

I went to school the next day sporting a huge black eye that looked like a big black plum. I was standing around in the yard squinting through one eye when Ernie catches sight of me. He walks over to me, points at my eye and asks, "Who's done that?" I don't answer, telling tales is not the curriculum at school. A little lad burst in, "Biffa," he says "Smashed him straight int eye because he'd had a feight wiv dare youg un."

"I'll fuckin 'Biffa' him," says Ernie, and promptly seeks out 'Biffa'. Ernie confronts him by asking, "Why dunt tha pick on somebody thi own size?" 'Biffa' replies, "Oh argh who?" He was clearly not intimidated by Ernie. In a flash Ernie counters, "Me," then thumps 'Biffa' in the eye. Straight away 'Biffa' throws a punch back, a full blown fight breaks out between the two, not a roll about on the floor, but a punch for punch proper fight. Crowds of kids gather round with the usual chant, "A FEIGHT." "A FEIGHT." "A FEIGHT". A couple of teachers split them up and march them off.

Our teacher follows behind the foursome. We were all seated in the classroom by the time Taffy entered. "Pass, to the front," he ordered. "Here," says Taffy pointing to me, "Is a typical bully, hits smaller people than himself, can't fight his own battles, so what does he do? He gets someone else to fight them for him, in other words a coward and a trouble causer." My mind in turmoil, my stomach in knots, stood before the whole class, I began to tremble involuntary. He cuts his speech short by saying, "Sit down Pass, you're pathetic." He was crucifying me at every opportunity and by the way he did it, it felt as if he was using screws not nails.

On the Friday of that week I had the fortune to have some bad luck. Playing football I twisted one way my boot studs stuck in the turf kept my knee facing the other. The result was twisted knee ligaments. The pain was excruciating, I was taken to the Royal Infirmary to be strapped up.

The doctors orders were music to my ears, "Keep off your bad leg for six to eight weeks." So I made my way back home on crutches feeling pleased with myself at the prospect of no Burngreave School for two months.

During my absence from school I got bits and pieces of homework passed on to me by one of my classmates, always with an added message of get well from my teacher. My mother thought it was nice of him. Oh how I longed to be back in Martin Street.

By this time little Pete had died of meningitis and was buried in Burngreave Cemetery. I used to pass the cemetery on my way to Burngreave School, which was an added burden to my despair. During my time off I would wonder what wrong I'd done to be in a situation of despair at school. It seemed inconceivable even to a twelve year old that a teacher could be so vindictive. He had cut me off, set me apart from all forms of school life, mainly because of his overwhelming popularity. It couldn't be because of the rugby could it? He did seem ultra keen on sport. I suppose he was used to undying support, that my choice of football instead of rugby was seen as an outright act of defiance.

Whatever due to my total lack of self confidence,

which was reflected in my schoolwork, I felt more and more I was being drawn into a whirlpool of despair. The two months off school flashed by and I was back in Taffy's class with the customary sick note written by my mother.

I felt a slight twinge of optimism, a new start; he'll probably be less vindictive. I handed him the sick note, the first lesson English, Taffy stood up with the sick note and wrote on the blackboard an exact copy of my mother's note. Now he addressed the class, "Here we have a note from Fred's mother." He then went on to correct my mother's spelling mistakes, to a chorus of giggles from the class, I blushed up and the whirlpool of despair began whirling in my stomach. "Ho no," I wanted to cry, but you can't cry at twelve, I wanted to run home and tell my mam, you don't do that at twelve. I felt deep shame because I had these feelings. I sat in utter despair.

The maths lesson followed the English. Taffy wrote about ten fraction sums on the board and told us all to write down answers. As I'd been off sick I'd never seen a fraction before, so I brought it to Taffy's attention. "Right then Pass I will tell you the principals of fractions." He then went on as fast as he could for about thirty seconds, and then added get on with it. I'd not understood a word of what he was saying, I was totally dumfounded. I don't know how I offered any sort of answers but when he came to mark my paper he drew my attention by saying, "Pass," he then tore my paper in half and dropped it in the waste bin.

Humiliation was his game. Due to his skit at my mother's spelling, I decided to avoid the playground at dinner time, it was sure to be a place of trouble. He was cutting me adrift by his skits and comments. I felt ashamed of myself; I felt a coward, long trousers and all. It was forbidden to stand around in the corridors at dinnertime but I thought I'd risk it.

I was stood in the vicinity of the headmaster's office one day, outside the office was a large gong, the head used to bash it a couple of times to indicate times up, on hearing this the whistleblowers on yard duty would go through their whistle blowing routine.

This day I'm hanging around, and this big blond haired lad dashes up, picks up the gong and sends it crashing down the concrete steps causing all sorts of bedlam. On releasing it, he's off like a flash.

Confused I don't know what to do so I decide on nothing; if I run it will be a sort of admission of guilt so I stand motionless. Within seconds I'm surrounded by teachers including the head. "You boy," bellows the head, "Did you do that?" "No sir," Taffy chips in, "The fact that you are in the corridor is against school rules." Which was a bit rich coming from a bloke who from time to time would announce to the class that he was having a sale, and sell exercise books, pencils and rulers all at below shop prices?

"Well," said the head, "If it wasn't you who was it?" "I don't know," I said obeying the first rule of any fifties school, don't tell tales. "You leave me with no alternative but to conclude it was you. In my office." He had an alternative, but that would have meant someone getting away with something, and that could not be seen to be done. I received two strokes of the cane.

As part of my punishment I had to report to the head every day after dinner. He provided me with a rag and a can of 'Brasso' to polish the gong. I had to perform this duty every day for a week. I would be sitting on the steps and the real culprit would walk by, ruffle my hair, and give me a wink in acknowledgement of me not shopping him. At least I thought I'd got a friend.

The following week was much like any other I was really in despair. Metalwork was done in a prefab sort of building, and at metalwork, choose what ever my state of mind, I was completely useless. As I had missed lessons due to my injury I was well behind the others. Our metalwork teacher was a much older bloke than all the other teachers. Grim faced, slightly hunched back, he was a cane em at every opportunity kind of bloke, and as I was useless at metalwork I would always give him the opportunity.

This particular day he had a technical drawing pinned to the blackboard. The drawing was done on paper with little squares on it. We all stood at our benches, all the other lads had part drawings done, my paper was blank due to the fact that I had been absent from school for two months. Two places to my right stood a little kid called Harry Bingham, a nice friendly kid who was about as good at metalwork as I. When I asked the teacher what I should do, he just replied, "Get on with it." On completion I was sure of one thing; my drawing looked nothing like his.

He slowly walked around the respective benches, mumbling comments to different pupils. When he got to Harry he did not say a word but drew back his clenched fist and punched Harry in the back of the head sending him sprawling. Christ, I thought, wait till he sees my drawing. I did not have to wait long; crack, a similar punch hit me on the neck, I was propelled sideways a couple of yards. I suddenly snapped, "I'm going," I said and made a dash for the door, I shouted, "Come on Harry lets fuck off."

Harry was quickly behind me and we were dashing across the playground towards the locked gates. The teacher made no attempt to chase us but stood with his hands on his aproned hips shouting, "Get back here at once." I was quickly over the gate encouraging Harry, "Come on, come on." Harry's face was pitiful, "Ah dern't Fred, am sorry." Harry stood school side gripping the iron bars of the gate looking full of worry. "Its alreight Harry," I said and off I ran back home to Boyland Place. Escape from Alcatraz.

I dashed into our house and blurted out, "Teachers hit me, am not going back." My mother was startled by my sudden appearance, "Look at ya neck a can see he as, what teacher?" "Metalwork bloke," I said. Quick as a flash she puts her coat on saying, "I'll give him chuffin metalwork, come on." "Am not goin back." "Oh yes you are," she said.

Within twenty minutes my mam and me are standing outside the head teacher's door. The head was expecting us, "Come in please Mrs. Pass," my mother

126

straight on the attack, points to my neck and says, "Look at this lot." "Yes, I can see," said the head, "It seems to be an unfortunate incident, and the teacher in question realises he's probably overstepped the mark. I do hope you realise that teachers are subjected to an awful lot of pressure at times." "Don't talk chuffin rubbish," my mother counted, "My husbands had years of working just to put bread ont table, so tha knows what tha can do wi that tale." The head says, "Let Fred take the rest of the day off and we can put this unfortunate incident behind us."

"Iz not coming back" says me mam, "And that's final." "You do realise," says the head, "He has to have an education by law?" "Yes," says my mother, "and I hope you realise that teachers are forbidden by law to punch kids. So you find him another school, or I'm straight down to the Education people and they'll get to know about this lot." "Mm," mused the head, "I've taken the trouble to talk to Fred's class teacher. Apparently he has a record of bullying and trouble causing, plus his schoolwork leaves a lot to be desired." "All chuffin lies," says me mam, "Iz sick every morning before coming to school."

At this the head asked us to wait outside while he made a phone call. After a few minutes he called us both back in. "I've had a word with the head of Hillfoot School and he's willing to take Fred on." "Right," said me mam, "I hope you've not given him a bad name, with all that trouble causing rubbish." "No, Mrs. Pass I have not, Fred will start with a clean slate."

On our way back home I felt utter relief at not

having to ever go back to Burngreave School. My mother sent me to the shops just before teatime. I bumped into Ernie Fearnehough, "Did a runner dint tha?" "Argh," I said, Ernie then said, "Doz tha want to come wi uz tut 'Empire' tonight, were goin to see Al Martino?" Al Martino was an American-Italian crooner of the time who had just had a number one hit with 'Here in my heart'.

The 'Empire', a wondrous place, was where you could actually see people who you had only heard on radio. I'd been many times to see radio stars such as Billy Cotton, George Formby, Tex Ritter, Nat Jackley, and Freddie Frinton.

Anyway it is 1954 and I'm sitting in the gods with Ernie and his mates. I'm still sporting a bit of a black eye, by courtesy of 'Biffa', plus a bit of a stiff neck, but for the first time in ages I felt a huge relief at not having butterflies in my stomach. Al Martino looked a lot smaller than I'd imagined and was dressed in a striking blue suit. He nevertheless brought the house down with his singing. He closed his act with his latest recording 'Wanted'. Boy could he sing.

Chapter 13

Hillfoot

So at the age of twelve I'm standing in the headmaster's office at my fourth school, Hillfoot County. Hillfoot School stood in a hollow just off Neepsend Lane. Like most schools of the time the main building was Victorian, which shouted out, 'house of correction'. The school had a square open tarmac'd playground. To the right as you entered through the main gates was a prefab style building with about ten steps in the middle that separated two classes. The prefab building was a later edition to the school, no doubt hastily erected to accommodate additional kids when the school leaving age went up from fourteen to fifteen.

To one side stood a large slag heap where nearby Andrews Toledo deposited unwanted material. High up behind the school was the Parkwood Springs Estate and Andrews Toledo's Spring Department ran down one side of the school. Along the front of the school ran the River Don adjacent to which ran a road come track, known locally as 'The Waterside'. With the presence of the slag heap the school would have been more aptly named 'Slagfoot', but then I suppose Hillfoot had a better ring to it.

The head's office stood right at the top of the building, me and me mam had to go up what seemed like a never ending spiralling concrete, castle like, well worn staircase. The head teacher was a smart dressed bespectacled bloke, with wavy hair and an engaging smile. Pleasantries were exchanged with me mam, and she left with the assurance that I would be alright.

In the distance I could hear the assembly in full voice singing 'Onward Christian Soldiers'. When my mother had left, the head Mr. Simmons looked me in the eyes and said, "Your headmaster from Burngreave has been in touch, so I'm fully aware of all the trouble you have caused at his school. I will tell you now Pass, the same principles apply at this school, as the ones at Burngreave, so any incidents of bullying, or trouble causing will be dealt with promptly, are you taking this in?" I nodded in reply. So much for the Burngreave School head's promise that I'd be starting with a clean slate.

Three words sprang to mind, the first two were frying pan, the other fire. The most striking thing I noticed about Mr. Simmons was his steely eyes; he seemed to look straight through you. "Come along Pass, I will introduce you to your new teacher and classmates." As I entered my new classroom the first thing I noticed was that it was mixed, boys and girls. The class was made up of about twenty of each sex, seated in couples of a boy and girl.

My new teacher was Mr. Perry, a small slim bloke with brown hair and a bushy moustache. As I settled into my new class Mr. Perry said, "Before I read the register will you all get out your history books and lift your ink container out of its well." After doing this a lad called

Carrigan was told to go round and fill the inkwells. Carrigan had a watering type can which held the watered down ink powder, mine was one of the first to be filled.

About halfway through the register I felt a tug on the back of my hair, I ignored it, then another tug, then another. I moved my arm back to indicate stop it. Then all of a sudden there was a loud scream, from the tugger, a girl called Shirley Mosley. "What's going on?" said Mr. Perry. Shirley said, "He's knocked my ink well all over my history book." My arm movement had caused the spillage. "Right," said Mr. Perry, "out to the front Pass."

I stood at the front on my very first day at my new school. Mr. Perry said, "I've not got through the register and by now you are causing trouble." I was too overcome by the situation to explain it was an accident and by previous experience I thought it pointless anyway. "Hold out your hand," he demanded, whack down came the cane.

What a chuffin start. All the kids in the class were very friendly, so apart from the inkwell incident the school seemed a very friendly place. As the first day of school was coming to an end, our head teacher entered the classroom, and my heart sank as Mr. Simmons said in a loud voice, "And how's the new boy settling in Mr. Perry?" To my utter relief and total surprise Mr. Perry said, "Oh he's doing fine." To which Mr. Simmons said, "Good lad, good lad," and left. I couldn't believe it. He could have easily given me a bad name over the inkwell incident, but didn't. Mr. Perry probably didn't realise it, but his actions earned him my utmost respect.

Back at home in 1954, due to my brother Brian working down the coal mine at Treeton, we had a radiogram, the ultimate, bar for television, in home entertainment. It looked a lovely piece of furniture, made out of polished walnut. You could get the radio stations without the customary squeaks and squeals that our old wireless gave out. Also you could get Radio Luxembourg, and listen to the top twenty and shows like the 'Jack Jackson Show'. Radio Luxembourg seemed, in contrast to the BBC, more modern, and you could hear all the latest record releases from such as Johnnie Ray, and Frankie Laine. The BBC in comparison sounded much more formal.

In no time we had a collection of records, many were of Al Jolson due to the popularity of two films 'The Jolson Story' and 'Jolson Sings Again'. I was amazed that on our radiogram we could play twelve records in one session.

I palled in with a lad at school called Tony Chapman, a blond haired lad who in the main was up for owt. We used to mooch about on Neepsend Lane after school and chat away on all sorts of subjects. It was strange in a way that we were pals. Tony's sport was swimming, I was scared to death of water, and even at a young age Tony was practical, liked messing with cars and good at woodwork, where as I could not tell one end of a screwdriver from the other. We'd walk along Neepsend Lane, at times, due to the pollution bellowing out of all the steelworks, you could not see a hand in front of you. Sometimes there was thick orange smog that hung about for ages, it had a repugnant smell and always left you with a bad taste in your mouth. You could hear the tram car coming but not see it due to the pollution.

One evening we stood on Hillfoot Bridge and I noticed a lad of about seventeen standing with his arms crossed, he wore a sort of menacing expression. He was only about five foot six, and not particularly well built, but never the less looked menacing by his stance. "Who's that?" I asked Tony. "Oh that's Paddy," Tony said, "keep well away." "What's he stood there for?" I counted. "He's looking for a feight, stands there all night. If any one looks twice at him, that's it, crash, bang, wallop. So if you ever have to pass him just say, "Alreight Paddy."

One night we'd about two bob apiece and nowt to spend it on, when Tony comes up with an idea, "Lets try and get in 'Fred Holmes'." 'Fred Holmes' was a dance hall at the top of Wood Street; the only snag was that you had to be sixteen to get in. Tony said, "We'll just lie about our age and blag our way in." So off we went.

To enter 'Fred Holmes' you had to go up steep steps to reach the dance hall. At the bottom of the steps stood a bouncer complete with tuxedo, a six foot tub of lard, with about as much humour and compassion. "Were you goin?" he asked as we tried to squeeze past. "For a dance," says Tony. "Oh, no you're not," says the bouncer adding, "Ya not owd enough." Instinctively I said, "We are." To which the bouncer gives me a great slap across the face with the flat of his hand. It was like getting slapped with a plank of wood. The whole of Wood Street was spinning as we walked back disconsolate.

As we got to the bottom of the street Tony was commiserating with me. We were, between us, contemplating getting our own back. All of a sudden Paddy barks, "What's up wi him?" Tony says, "Chuffin bouncer at 'Fred Holmes' az give him a slap." To which Paddy says, "Come on, I'll sort him out." As Paddy marches up Wood Street we follow a couple of yards behind.

As large as life Paddy walks up to the bouncer who towered above him, hitches his trousers up with his elbows Cagney style, and says indicating to me with his thumb behind him. "Az tha just hit him?" "Argh" says the bouncer, "And if tha dunt shift thi sen, thal get one n'all." "Go on then," says Paddy, and the bouncer swings the flat of his hand in Paddy's direction. Paddy blocks the swing with his left arm, leaps up and punches the bouncer flush on the chin, the bouncer begins to fall forward like a freshly cut tree, only before he hits the ground Paddy gives him a right, then a left to the face with lightning proficiency. Thud, the bouncer hit the deck. It felt like an earth tremor on Wood Street. As he lay unconscious Paddy snarls, "Useless twat," and gives him a couple of kicks in the ribs for good measure.

Paddy looked quite satisfied with his nights work, turned to us and said, "You two, piss off." We were just a means to an end and now no further use to him. So after the events of that evening Tony's words of, "Just say, alreight Paddy," sounded good advice.

In comparison to Burngreave, Hillfoot was a joy.

I'd got a mate Tony, my teacher Mr. Perry made going to school a pleasure, so all in all things were looking up. I used to like writing, but noticed when my work was marked Mr. Perry emphasized my spelling mistakes by circling them with a red biro. I was, and still am, terrible at spelling. So I did one composition with the words I couldn't spell, substituted with words I could. When marking this particular essay Mr. Perry called me to his desk and said, "This is a right load of tosh Pass. I usually like reading your stuff, but not this." His words, "I usually like reading your stuff," was music to my ears. It was praise and although a little back handed still praise, something I'd been starved of.

I explained the spelling angle, to which he replies, "Write it again, and forget your spelling problem. Writing is a form of expression, so write it again, only this time with flair." I couldn't wait to get into it; I was like a dog let off a leash in a big open space. I re-wrote the essay and presented it to him.

He said, "Excellent, take it to the head and tell him I've sent you." So it was with some pride that I knocked on Mr. Simmon's door, "Enter," he called. I duly handed over the manuscript. He sat frowning whilst reading my work. He then jumped up and said, "No wonder Mr. Perry has sent you to me, your spellings atrocious, hold out your hand," and promptly caned me.

On getting back to the class Mr. Perry enquired, "What's the head said?" I replied, "He's given me the cane because of all the spelling mistakes." "Oh dear, I'm sorry about that Pass he's obviously got the wrong end of the stick." "No," I said, "it's me that's got wrong end of stick." Mr. Perry chuckled and said, "I suppose your right, sit down Pass, remember this incident, you may be able to use it in your future writing. Then at least you've got some thing out of the situation."

Kids being kids are mischievous. One winter's day we all sat down in class and a lad called Lenny Askham sat wearing a balaclava. For a laugh he was wearing it back to front, his face was completely covered up with the hole at the back of his head. Giggles began to break out, we all wondered how Mr. Perry would react when realising the situation. Lenny sat for about twenty minutes supposedly reading a book. As the giggles got louder Mr. Perry looked up and said, "What's all the laughing about?" Then catching sight of Lenny said, "Stand up please Askham." Askham stood up. Mr. Perry with a stunted smile on his face said, "For your benefit Askham, take off your balaclava," which Lenny then did. Mr. Perry went on, "You wear it with the hole at the front, so there I've taught you something, pretty basic stuff but nevertheless, taught you something."

He then went on, "How old are you Askham?" "Nearly thirteen," replied Lenny. "Well," said Mr. Perry, "In Dickensian times", he then stopped, "No, I'll not go down that road," he changed his track. "Many years ago boys of your age were being pushed up chimneys with a brush attached to their heads. No education, just hard unyielding dirty work. How would you like that?" Lenny answered, "It sounds a good job to me sir." "I'm sure it does," said Mr. Perry, "I'm sure it does, sit down now Askham and stop messing about."

Another funny situation arose when three of us were put on corridor duty, Tony, a lad nicknamed 'Spud', and me. Our duties involved standing at intervals to oversee the kids entering the classrooms in an orderly manner. By now Tony, 'Spud', and me were smokers so we didn't mind the corridor duty. We would enjoy a fag, as we'd enrolled a younger kid on lookout so that we could then puff away.

One day, the corridor we were in was full of smoke from our cigarettes when the alarm went up. "PERRY'S HERE," we could hear his footsteps; Tony flicked the fag out of the window. 'Spud' in a panic ran into the empty classroom, by the side of the teacher's desk was a large wicker basket, in he jumped closing the lid behind him.

"Good god," Mr. Perry said, "Have you been smoking?" We replied in unison, "No sir." "Well the school must be on fire then. Do you know?" he went on, "Smoking's a daft, mucky chuffin habit?" we both nodded in agreement and nothing else was said.

To our horror Mr. Perry sat at his desk and it was obvious he wasn't going to move. On resumption of the afternoon's schoolwork, he asked, "Where's Johnson?" Somebody straight away said, "Ah think he's gone home sick sir," Tony and me were wondering how 'Spud' was going to get out of the situation. He was in the basket right besides the teacher's desk.

It got to about 3 o'clock when a girl from another class entered our classroom. "Our teacher says can we have the P.T. ribbons?" "Yes, help your self," he said pointing to the basket. The girl opens the basket and jumps back giving a scream, and out pops 'Spud'. "Oh my god," says Mr. Perry, "What on earth are you doing in the basket?" 'Spud' replies, "I was tired so I thought I'd have a lie down, ah must have dropped off."

"Johnson," he said, "The next time the circus is in town you might apply for a job as magician's assistant! We've got Askham who thinks being pushed up chimneys is a good job, and now Johnson practising to be a magician's apprentice. To think I've given up a job in industry to teach you lot."

It was around this time that I used to go to a youth club named 'The Helen Wilson Settlement'. A bloke who helped there had an idea to start a boxing club. I mentioned it to my dad, who thought it would be a good idea for me to join, considering the black eye I'd acquired whilst at Burngreave.

He went on to tell me about when he was a young man, and how he and his brothers used to spend many a Sunday afternoon, fighting each other with bear knuckles. I thought, I'd have thought of something more pleasant than that. From the age of about five my dad had always preached the basic principles of boxing to me. "Always stand sideways on, that way you reduce the target to your opponent. Keep your elbows tucked in therefore protecting your kidneys. Keep your chin on your chest because, choose who you are, you'll go down if you are punched on the chin."

Well armed with these principles I attended the boxing club. It all seemed so easy against kids who were just taking up the sport, and I seemed to be knocking kids over for fun. I must have been a bit cocky because one day the bloke who ran the boxing club said, "Get here for 7pm on Friday Fred, I've got a kid coming down and I want you to show him how to go on." "No problem," I said thinking to myself, if he's only learning the job I'd not be too hard on him. I told my dad who said, "I might come and have a look."

Come Friday and I enter the youth club to see a proper ring erected and full of people. I think to myself, just the job, just think of the glory. In fact a perfect set up to show off my two or three weeks boxing experience. I was growing all the time so for my age I was tall, but skinny. The muscles in my arms looked like knots in cotton. I looked across the ring at my opponent. He was a dark haired good looking kid, smaller than me but perfectly formed. Ah well, shame about me about to change his looks, but he'll just have to do his best.

Clang, the bell went for round one, out dances my opponent. I walk towards him then bop, bam, bop, bop; he hits me four times before I can blink. Right, I think to myself, he's asked for it I'm not going to take it easy on him. I lunge forward, he sways to one side then he hits me about six times in the time it takes to blink an eye. I rush at him swinging my arms but he's not there, I spin round to face him bop, bang, wallop, bop. I can't get anywhere near him. Clang, end of round one and I've not hit him yet. On punches connected I'm trailing about one hundred and forty to nil. His punches aren't actually hurting, but they're not doing me any good that's for sure. I'm sitting in my corner gasping for breath totally bemused. I look across at my opponent and he's looking a bit bored by the situation. The bloke in my corner who is giving me advice says, "Get him in a corner so he can't bob and weave. Give him what for."

Clang, round two, I manage to get my arms around him and sort of wrestle him into a corner, then I let fly bash, clang, wallop. I have my eyes shut in desperation as I throw these punches, I open them to find I've been hitting the ring post not my opponent. I spin round to face a ten punch barrage that has the onlookers applauding in appreciation, clang, and the end of round two. My breathing by now is reaching critical proportions. My dad pops his head through the ropes and asks me a question. "You are showing Him how to go on?" he then said, "You got him worried that round Fred he though he was killing you." As I stood up for round three I was out of breath, my arms and legs felt like jelly, my nose was running, my eyes were running and I was wondering what I was going to do to survive another round.

The third round was just a continuation of the other two; I think I managed to give a glancing blow to his shoulder, which only geed him up to throw another dozen blows back, each blow spot on. After about thirty seconds of the third round the referee mercifully called the fight to a halt. I've hesitated before I used the word fight; I should have said, stopped him hitting me.

Then a bloke jumps into the ring and announces as he holds the other kids arm up, "Ladies and gentlemen, a round of applause please for Johnnie Fitzpatrick, Yorkshire's West Riding schoolboy champion." As I made my way back to the broom cupboard style room that had been used as a dressing room, I hear the bloke go on to say, "And Johnnie has very kindly agreed to put on an exhibition of skipping for us." I slump down on my chair still breathless, desperately trying to suck air. Through the open door I can see Johnnie skipping forwards, backwards, cross armed and all sorts of tricks to the tune of Georgia Brown. I thought I'll get changed and slip off so no one notices me leaving.

To get my gloves off I pull the laces with my teeth. Dam I had only succeed in pulling the lace into a knot. I desperately pull at the other glove using the same method, the same thing happens. So I can't go any where, I have to sit through half an hour of watching Johnnie performing his skipping tricks.

When he had completed his exhibition of skipping Johnnie came into the dressing room and said, "Oh you still here Fred?" On seeing my predicament with the gloves he said, "Oh lets give you a hand." While we were both getting dressed I asked Johnnie, "Are you sure you're not the English schoolboy champion?" To which he replied, "Oh no, that's so and so, he's much better than me." "Yorkshire champion?" I queried. "No, no I've a long way to go before I get as good as him," he said modestly.

As we parted outside the club Johnnie said, "All the best Fred, we'll have to do it again sometime." A real nice kid he was. I said, "Yeah," but was thinking not if I can chuffin help it. The last I heard of Johnnie was that he'd emigrated to Australia, South Africa or somewhere but I never heard of him making a name for himself in boxing. Despite his obvious superiority over me he conducted himself, both through and after the fight, like a true sportsman. He did not showboat, pull faces or do somersaults after he had won. He did his best to leave me with a bit of dignity. As for me, I decided to stick to football. You know what; my nose has started to bleed, whilst writing about Johnnie Fitzpatrick.

After being in the ring with Johnnie I was convinced that sometime in the far off future, Johnnie would become an all time great of boxing and I'd be able to tell my grandkids of the time we shared the same ring. For Johnnie it wasn't to be, Sheffield born football manager, Jim Smith tells in his book that his first love was boxing but decided on football after fighting...... yes you've guessed it.... Johnnie Fitzpatrick!

Chapter 14

Mr. Feinburg

So after the first year at Hillfoot, I left Mr. Perry's class in the main building of the school, to continue my education in the prefab style building in the school yard. For the last two years boys were separated from the girls. I think the idea behind it was if we were not separated at that age we would start to breed.

What made it hard for teachers was that they would not have one class of forty, but twenty boys in their penultimate year and twenty boys in their final year. Therefore the teacher was in effect teaching two classes at once. Add to this the same teacher taught everything with the exception of P.T. and woodwork, quite a job.

Our teacher in the prefab was Mr. Feinberg, who reputedly had a quick temper, and was supposed to be of Russian origin. Mr. Feinberg was a small plumpish bloke with a moustache and receding hairline. His hair was wiry and curly and seemed to grow out wild and sideways similar in style to Albert Einstein. His trousers seemed a little short in the leg. His jacket seemed too small and he always had the middle button fastened. The jacket was so tight you got the impression of the button bursting free and taking out someone's eye.

The girls were in the same kind of set up, in the same building yet in a separate classroom and taught by a pleasant lady called Miss Whitham.

An amusing incident happened one day after Mr. Feinberg announced that our class was to go on a trip to the waterworks. It was hardly a heart stopping event looking at water being refined, but nevertheless a change from being cooped up in a classroom that was freezing in winter, and boiling hot in summer.

At break time a lad in our class, John Whittaker, said quite casually, "I'll not be going, I've things to do." John who's nickname was 'Buster', was a ginger haired stocky lad who wore dark framed glasses. 'Buster' was well known for his handyman activities. He had stick rounds, would go on all sorts of errands, whitewash outside toilets in fact do anything that would earn him a bob or two.

A double decker Sheffield Transport bus was hired for the occasion, so with 'Buster's' earlier comments it was no surprise when he didn't turn up. As the bus trundled on Neepsend Lane, all the bus load of kids gave out a great cheer at the sight of 'Buster' with his home made barrow sauntering along Neepsend Lane.

On spotting him Feinberg shouted to the driver, "STOP THE BUS." The bus screeched to a halt. On seeing this 'Buster' turned his barrow upside down and hid under it tortoise style. Mr. Feinberg was furious; he stood on the platform of the now stationary bus and shouted, "WHITTAKER COME OUT, YOU'VE BEEN SEEN." No movement at all from the tortoise, "COME OUT WHITTAKER," still no movement. By this time there was pandemonium on the bus with all of the kids chanting,

"'BUSTER', 'BUSTER', 'BUSTER'." The bus driver started to get agitated by all the noise and shouted to Mr. Feinberg, "AH WE GOOIN TUT WATERWORKS OR WHAT?" To which Mr. Feinberg replied, clearly exasperated, "Oh, drive on, drive on."

The day at the waterworks turned out just as expected, how do you keep forty kids interested in looking at water in different levels of purification? As we queued to get in Mr. Feinberg went off to find who was in charge. As we stood there someone noticed a frog. It was in the centre of a big round circle of what looked like mud being sprinkled with water continually through a tube which slowly circled the mud. At the side of this was a pile of coke fuel, someone threw a coke to try to make the frog jump. By the time Mr. Feinberg returned the pile of coke had disappeared, the mud cake was covered in cokes and the frog had never moved.

Next day, before lessons commenced, Mr. Feinberg announced, "Whittaker stand up please, would you kindly tell me and the class what you were doing pushing a barrow on Neepsend Lane yesterday afternoon when you should have been with us on our trip to the waterworks?" "Ah weren't on Neepsend Lane sir," replied 'Buster'. "Don't tell lies, Whittaker. I confronted you and you disappeared under your barrow like a tortoise."

All the class laughed, to which Mr. Feinberg snapped, "SHUDUP." Come on boy explain yourself. "It weren't me," insisted 'Buster'. By now Mr. Feinberg was getting madder and madder. "Don't lie to me boy, you were seen. I was closer to you yesterday than I am now." "It weren't me and that's all thi iz to it," said 'Buster'. "Right," said Mr. Feinberg, "I will conduct this enquiry like a court of law. I am the prosecutor, and you are the accused. Does that seem reasonable Whittaker?" To which he replied, "You can do what you want, but it weren't me."

Mr. Feinberg was warming to the idea of a mock court case. "Well we will do this democratically. Whittaker, you will be tried by your very own." He walked over to the window looking out with his back to the class and said in a casual sort of way, "Hands up all who saw Whittaker on Neepsend Lane yesterday afternoon."

When he turned round he was aghast at what he saw, not one hand was raised. Blood red in the face he shouted out names at random, "Ward did you see Whittaker?" "No sir," was the reply. "Toothill, did you see Whittaker? "No sir." He went through about ten potential witnesses then finally gave up the ghost by saying, "Sit down Whittaker, because of your industrial nature you'll probably end up a millionaire, and I'll end up in the madhouse." At break time I said to 'Buster', "Ya gorra way wi that John," to which he replied, "It weren't me anyway."

When it came to avoiding being in the classroom Tony and I were always at the forefront of volunteers. One day Mr. Feinberg announced, "There is to be a trip to the City Hall to see the Hallé Symphony Orchestra." He was reading the details off a paper and without looking up he said, "Put your hand down Chapman, and put your hand down Pass." As we were putting our hands down he looked up, he had a wry smile on his face, he just knew our hand would be the first up. He then went on, "I will be taking down names of pupils who wish to attend. The rules are, once I have taken your names the agreement that you will go to the concert will be, to coin a phrase, 'set in concrete', do you understand." There were a few mumbles. He then practically picked out Tony and me by saying, "Chapman," Tony nodded. "Pass," I did likewise. I was thinking no doubt the same as Tony, What's he on about? Who's going to change there minds on spending an afternoon in the classroom as opposed to an afternoon at the City Hall. Mr. Feinberg then called each boys name out requiring a yes or no.

When he had completed his list he announced to our horror, "Right then we all meet at school at 6pm, on Tuesday of next week." Straight away two hands went up, I hadn't a clue what my excuse would be, but like Tony there was no way I was going to spend my off school time listening to the Hallé Orchestra. "Just as I thought," said Mr. Feinberg. "Stand up Chapman, stand up Pass. Yes," he said to Tony, "What do you want to tell me Mr. Chapman?" "Ah can't go," said Tony. "And why not?" retorted Mr. Feinberg. "Er, er." "Come on Chapman out with it." "Am having swimming lessons on Tuesday night," said Tony. "You mean one to one lessons, your own personal trainer Chapman?" Mr. Feinberg countered. The class began to giggle but Tony was unmoved. "Yes," he replied, "My mother insists on it." "It's not anyone famous who trains you Chapman is it, not Johnny Weissmuller I take it?" "No sir," said Tony. Feinberg was trying to embarrass Tony, but I knew Tony would be unmoved. Feinberg finally relented by saying, "By all accounts you are a good swimmer Chapman. So if these lessons do exist in reality, I suppose it's some sort of education, the physical kind." While he was grilling Tony my mind was doing gymnastics, searching for a reason to avoid the City Hall, I could not use the swimming angle I couldn't swim.

So I was totally nonplussed when Feinberg said, "Now then Mr. Pass why can't you attend?" I stammered, "Er rum, Er rum, Errr." "Come on Pass lets hear it." Without putting any thought into it I suddenly blurted out, "Ave got to look after house." Mr. Feinberg seized on my comment like a spider catching a fly. His eyes literally lit up, "Why?" he asked. I knew I was in for a grilling. "Because me mother works at evening and me dad and brother work shifts."

"You have to look after the house?" said Mr. Feinberg. He now stood like he was a QC at the Old Bailey. "Do you live in a mobile home?" he asked. "Ah what?" I replied. "You're not from gypsy stock Pass are you, live in a caravan that could be hooked up and whisked away in a flash?" All the class started laughing, "No sir." "Where do you live Pass?" asked Mr. Feinberg. "Boyland Place," I said. "That's just off Neepsend Lane isn't it?" "Yes." "Have you priceless paintings adorning your walls?" "No sir." "Or perhaps large quantities of jewellery?" "No sir, but me mother alus likes me int house on Tuesday nights."

I was squirming inside but there was no way I was

going to the City Hall and I wanted to be with my pal Tony. Still he would not let up, "How long have you lived on Boyland Place?" "About four years sir." "Hmm, and during those four years how many houses have been moved brick by brick?" "Er, er, non sir." The 'class' were laughing their heads off at the cross examination, I wasn't bothered. Mr. Feinberg then closed proceedings by saying, "It crossed my mind to put your excuse to the vote of the class, but considering the Whittaker experience, it would be pointless. Sit down, you are excused." As I sat down Tony gave me the thumbs up. Due to the class laughing at us Tony said, "Well go and take the mickey out of all the kids that are going."

So come Tuesday, Tony and I scaled the perimeter wall and looked down on this line of lads. They all looked like scraped carrots and as miserable as sin. There did not appear to be a teacher in sight, so Tony and I began giving them 'some'. "Dozy twats," we shouted, and sarcastically "Ave a good time," all the time laughing our heads off. We slid down the wall, turned and bumped into Mr. Feinberg. "Ah, then Chapman and Pass, no swimming lessons or house sitting?" then without waiting for an answer he said, "By my desk in the morning."

We both got the cane the next day for, as Mr. Feinberg described, loutish behaviour. But we weren't bothered, as far as we were concerned we'd won, or at least drawn.

Chapter 15

The box – The Bike – Dennis Hobson

I arrived home from school one evening in 1955 to witness our house full of people, Mother, Dad, Brother Brian, and Uncle Ernest. They were all sitting staring at a box in the corner of the room, our very first television set. "What's for tea?" I asked. "Shh," said my mother, "I'll do you something soon." "Come and have a look at this, bloody marvellous," my dad said, "Tha can't believe it can tha?" his eyes transfixed to the telly. "No tha can't," chipped in Uncle Ern, "Wiv come a long way since cat's whiskers." There was then complete silence, what was the programme that had commanded their total attention and amazement? 'Muffin the Mule'.

When the programme ended the announcer declared, "There will now be an intermission," and a picture came up of a windmill with its blades slowly going round. Across the screen was a caption that read, 'Interlude'. Nobody moved until my dad broke the silence by saying, "This'll not do. I'll have to get back to work." With the Hallamshire being close by it meant he could nip home during break times. Off he went singing under his breath, 'Here comes Muffin, Muffin the Mule'.

We had the ultimate home entertainment for 1955, our very own telly. We had a television cover; for someone told my mother if you covered the screen with a cover when the TV was not in use, it would improve the quality of the picture. In no time at all we had what the shops described as a television lamp. By having a TV lamp on the top of your set, it was said to improve the lustre of the vision. These TV lamps came in all sorts of guises. Ours was a multi coloured fish with a visible little light bulb inside it. Our fish had a particularly gormy look, a sort of, 'What am I, a fish doing on top of a telly?' sort of expression.

I remember the imported American programmes being the best. These were mostly on I.T.V., and included 'Amos and Andy', 'I married Joan', and a kids favourite, 'The Lone Ranger'. Clayton Moore played the Lone Ranger; his sidekick was Tonto who was played by a real American Indian called Jay Silverheels. Tonto always addressed the Lone Ranger by the name Kemosabe. A television related joke went round school. "Why did the Lone Ranger shoot Tonto?" "I don't know why did the Lone Ranger shoot Tonto?" "Because he found out Kemosabe means sweetheart." The best BBC programmes were 'The Grove Family', and 'Dixon of Dock Green', which were in general, a more staid type of programme. All the announcers talked posh and sounded as though they'd just nipped out from Buckingham Palace. The two I remember most were Sylvia Peters and McDonald Hobley.

At thirteen years old I always felt at a loose end as far as social activities were concerned, too old to go out with my parents, yet too young for pubs, dance halls and such things. So that just left the pictures on Friday nights, and watching 'Wednesday' on alternate Saturdays. I was a bit too young to be involved with girls for at thirteen my hormones were just doing stretching exercises.

So most evenings Tony and I would mooch around the district and usually end up sitting outside Mrs. Kenworthy's fruit shop at the bottom of Tony's road. Mrs. Kenworthy was a real nice old lady. Sometimes we would be joined by a few other classmates and we would sit around chatting on all sorts of subjects. Tony was a close neighbour of Mrs. Kenworthy, and many was the night she enquired from the closed darkened shop, "Is that you and your friends Tony?" Being as she was a nice old lady, Tony was, as we were, always respectful and would reply, "Yes, Mrs. Kenworthy." To which she'd answer, "OK Tony love, good night lads." I think she felt safer by our presence, but as always there was a fly in the ointment and it came in the shape of a Bobby.

Our informal chats used to last till about 10pm, then we'd split up and wander off home. Most Bobbys would stop and say, "Alright lads, what ya up to?" Someone would reply, "Just chatting," then the lawman would pedal off with a parting comment like, "Just behave yourselves," which seemed to us a fair comment. But one particular Bobby would trundle up and start off by saying, "You lot, shift yersen." Tony would come back with, "We know owner of shop, and she likes us to sit here." To which he'd retort, "Well I don't, move it. Go on, do one, shift." So we'd split up and wander about, which narked us all for we were doing no harm. He was the only one to move us on and take pleasure in doing it. After moving us on he'd park his bike up, and disappear into the police box that was situated on Hillfoot Bridge.

Tony had the idea that we'd sit outside the 'Farfield' instead, so when 'PC 49', as Tony nicknamed him, turned up we'd have an excuse. When we were confronted outside the pub by this particular Bobby and told to move on, Tony replied, "We can't were waiting for our dads int pub." This narked the man in blue a bit, so he'd be off to his cop box with a parting comment like, "Well don't forget al be watching ya."

Tony and I were sitting outside the 'Farfield' one summer's evening when a lorry rolled up with smoke puthering out of the exhaust and making all sorts of unhealthy like noises. The bloke driving it jumps out leaving it parked skew whiff half blocking the road. On jumping out he didn't bother switching off the ignition, or indeed bother to close the cab door. He was a fit looking bloke probably in his early twenties. As he approached the pub he said, "Hiya lads," felt into his waistcoat pocket and flicked us both a two bob coin apiece with the comment, "If anyone wants to know who's wagon that is, tell em it's Dennis Hobson's, an am int pub if thi want mi. OK lads?" Two bob apiece we couldn't believe our luck.

Dennis Hobson was a well known hard man of the times. As far as street fighting was concerned, he was probably the uncrowned middleweight champion of Sheffield if not even further. His action of giving us two bob apiece had just acquired him two more fans.

After about ten minutes, who comes rolling along but the Bobby who always acted the hard man to us thirteen year old kids? He stopped his bike, and frowned as he looked at the obviously illegally parked lorry. It must in fact have been in contravention of about a dozen highway regulations. He did not bother about us being sat outside the pub; he'd got bigger fish to fry. He parked his bike, took out his notebook, flipped back the cover and began circling the vehicle, jotting down the registration as he did so. He was really giving the lorry the once over, running his hands over the tyres, making more notes. He examined the driver's side mirror, which promptly fell off. We both started laughing; the Bobby ignored this and carried on his examination. He must have half filled his book when he approached us for information, "Do ya know who owns this?" he asked. Still clutching our two bob apiece we were word perfect, and answered in unison, "Dennis Hobson and iz int pub if anybody wants im."

We were just thinking this'll be interesting. Then the Bobby without saying a word flipped back his notebook to close it, put it back into his top pocket, buttoned down the pocket, got back on his bike, pedalled over and then disappeared into the police box. He obviously didn't fancy telling Dennis to do one, or shift, like he did us. This was the same Bobby who had reputedly given kids a back hander for answering back. After about half an hour Dennis came out of the pub, he asked, "Any problems lads." To which, considering the two bob apiece, we replied, "No

Mr. Hobson." The Bobby, by his non action, was adding fuel to the fire as far as being not liked by the kids of the area, for Tony and I told everyone who was prepared to listen about the escapade.

A couple of weeks later we were sitting outside the 'Farfield'. 'PC 49' had pedalled past, completely ignored us and gone into his police box after parking his bike up, presumably to make himself a cup of tea. As we sat there a couple of school pals, who were a year or so older than us, came across Hillfoot Bridge in our direction. On seeing the bike parked up they stopped. They waved their hands in silence to catch our attention, then mimed to us while pointing with screwed up faces, "Is it him?" Tony and I nodded in the positive.

The two lads then tiptoed towards the bike, wheeled it to the other side of the bridge, lifted it and after a bit of a struggle dropped it into the River Don, then disappeared in the opposite direction. We being completely innocent sat our ground; in fact we looked forward to 'PC 49's' reaction.

Out he came, looked round frantically for his bike, went down the lane by the water, came back, looked all over the place but he never thought to look in the Don. Probably that's why he never made detective. Having exhausted all possible places, he looked over to us putting his helmet down. He came across, "Ave you seen anybody messin wi mi bike?" "Bike?" Tony queried. "Ah, bloody bike," the Bobby retorted, adding, "You two's not got owt to do with it ave ya?" We both shook our heads. "BLOODY,

Age 15 posing, soft chuff or what!

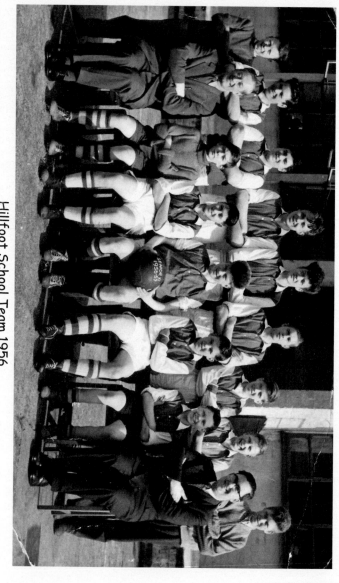

Hillfoot School Team 1956.

I am fifth left, back row. For interest, captain Jack Fowler later earned a living as part of a three man trapeze act known as Hunt, Lunt and Cunningham. Jack was Cunningham. They were later known as The Flying Delgadoes. Jack is pictured centre with ball. Extreme left, Headteacher Mr Simmons, extreme right, form teacher Mr Dowson.

CHUFFIN, TWATIN, BASTEREDIN, ELL," shouted the Bobby while looking up to the heavens. We both stood and Tony couldn't resist it, he said, "Tha can get done fo swearin tha noes," and with that we both legged it.

Chapter 16

'Big ADA'

As a little lad, my dad would often take me with him to the 'Rag and Tag' Market down Dixon Lane. On Dixon Lane were people selling fruit and flowers etc. on big flat barrows. They were parked down the right hand side of Dixon Lane facing the indoor Norfolk Market Hall. My dad would stop and chat to one of the fruit sellers. Her name was 'Big Ada'. As a little lad I found her a frightening figure, she was a big woman of about five feet nine, square shouldered, and solidly built, with huge hands and a deep fearful voice. She had a bloke that worked for her, doing the fetching and carrying, called Herbert. He scared me too, for he was a midget of about three foot six, with muscly arms. I'd never seen a midget before, and 'Little Herbert' as he was known scared the life out of me.

As a teenager in the fifties Dixon Lane became the place to be. For the fifties brought 'Rock n Roll', probably the first music to be aimed at teenagers. The likes of Elvis Presley, Little Richard, Jerry Lee Lewis and Chuck Berry would sound wild and lively compared to crooners such as Perry Como, Donald Peers, and Dickey Valentine. On top of this it was often derided by older people as rubbish and shocking, which made it even more appealing to teenagers.

Dixon Lane was the place to be because there was a music shop there called 'Canns', it sold records which could be heard blurting out non-stop. Lots of girls would be around the shop inside and out, so 'Canns' became a magnet for its music, and a good place to pick up lasses. Tony and I would often spend Saturday afternoons in and around 'Canns' chatting up girls.

We would sometimes go in and request a record on the pretence we were going to buy. We would say can I hear 'Be-Bop-Alula' by Gene Vincent and the counter assistant would tell you to go to one of three telephone box like booths, she would put on the record and the music would be transferred to your booth. After listening to it we would come out and say, "No thanks."

During an afternoon this would be repeated half a dozen times or so. So it was free music and as many girls to chat up as you wanted. Elvis Presley was the girls favourite, so with this in mind I tried to look as much like him as possible. Incredibly at fourteen I could grow sideburns, one of Elvis's trade marks, which was an advantage to make me look older than fourteen. I had confiscated an old coat of my brother's and had velvet put on the collar and cuffs so, with my drainpipe black jeans and two inch crepe sole shoes I was set up.

On one particular Saturday Tony, for some reason, didn't turn up, so I decided to have a chat to Ada. "Hiya Ada," I said as I approached, "How ya doin?" "HOW AM A DOIN?" Ada replied in her deep threatening voice, "THA LOOKS A REIGHT CHUFF IN THAT OUTFIT PASSY. DUNT HE HERBERT?" Looking up at me Herbert nodded in agreement and said, "Argh a reight chuff." "HOW'S THA

GOT IN THEM TROUSERS? POURED THI IN EM," went on Ada. Herbert chuckled, "Argh must ave poured thi in em." "WHATS THI DAD THINK OF THI DRESSED LIKE THAT?" Ada didn't wait for an answer and went on to ask, "HOW'S HE GOIN ON ANYWAY?" As I began to answer Ada didn't bother listening. Drowning me with her speil, "RIPEBANANAZFOURFORSIXABOBEIGHT." (Which translated meant, "Ripe bananas four for sixpence, and for a shilling you can have eight.")

She not only drowned me out, but all of the other traders on Dixon Lane, plus the sound of Elvis singing, 'All Shook Up' that was booming out of 'Canns'. Ada had all sorts of products on her barrow, lettuce, cabbages, bananas, apples and tomatoes. Under her barrow she had an old tin coffin shaped bath half full of water.

From time to time she'd say, "FRESHEN STALL UP HERBERT IT'S LOOKING AS SAD AS A RENT COLLECTOR." Herbert would soak a white cloth in the water, and then flick it over the stall bringing to life all the produce. A bloke walked up, and with finger and thumb began squeezing the tomatoes to check their solidity. Ada retorted in a loud voice, "DON'T SQUEEZE MI TOMATOES LUV, YA WUNT LIKE ME FUCKIN SQUEEZIN YOURS WOULD YA?" and then went on in an even more menacing shout to ask, "OR WOULD YA?" The bloke, not surprisingly, made his exit. 'Little Herbert' enjoyed Ada in full voice and said, "Ah don't think he wants his tomatoes squeezing Ada, ee, ee, ee."

Later that same afternoon a policeman came

walking slowly down Dixon Lane, hands behind his back, he walked with a kind of trepidation and for a second or two I wondered why. It soon became apparent when Ada swung into action. "THAT'S ALL WI WANT," and looking up through her eyebrows and with a fearsome expression on her face she went on, "AH WISH AH COULD GET PAID, TU STICK ME NOSE INTO OTHER PEOPLE'S BUSINESS." I was ready to leg it. Dixon Lane went quiet of chatter, in expectation of trouble. The sound of Bill Hayley singing, 'Rock Around the Clock' could be heard as clear as a bell coming out of 'Canns'. I'd no need to leg it, for the policeman looked up at the heavens as though inspecting the weather, started whistling, turned on his heels and slowly disappeared up the lane. Ada carried on her tirade by shouting after him, "GOO ON, GER OFF FUCKIN LANE."

Once he'd disappeared the lane was back to normality with people chatting, and vendors shouting their spiel. In full flight there was no one as fierce as Ada.

"Oh Ada," 'Little Herbert' said, "Ah wont be around Christmas time." "WHY?" demanded Ada. "Am in 'Snow White' at Bradford." "FUCK 'SNOW WHITE' THA WORKS FO ME." Ada's comment made me burst out laughing. 'Little Herbert' took umbridge to this and grabbed the back of my thigh in a vice like grip. "AAAARGH," I cried out in pain. Ada stepped in, "LERIM GU, YA LITTLE TWAT, LERIM GU." Herbert granted Ada's request and I breathed a sigh of relief, but I never got to know if Herbert got to Bradford or not.

Later in the day a nice looking girl of about sixteen came walking down the lane, Ada on noticing her said, "STOP HER FOR A CHAT PASSY." "Why? I asked. "JUST STOP HER," said Ada. As you can imagine I wasn't about to argue, so I swung into an old chat up line. I said to the girl as she approached. "Hiya love weren't you in the 'Wicker' pictures last night?" It was a chat up line because if they answered, "No", it meant you had no chance, but if they replied, "No, I always go to such and so pictures," you were in with a chance. You just took it from there, and Bob's your uncle you'd got a date. To my surprise this good looking girl answered, "No, I always go to the 'Scala' Saturday nights." My heart skipped a beat, I was about to follow this up with a, "What ya doin tonight?" question when Ada lifted her pinafore up and produced a huge cucumber and said to the girl, "AH BET YA WISH HE'D GOT ONE AS BIG AS THIS." The girl screeched, "Oh," and ran off down the lane, much to the amusement of 'Big Ada', and 'Little Herbert" who was holding his ribs consumed by laughter. Ada said, "NEER MIND PASSY THIZ MORE FISH INT SEA."

She then asked Herbert to go and find 'the time'; he came back with, "Nearly six," to which Ada declared, "THAT'S IT HERBERT, WRAP IT UP," meaning they were packing up for the day. Before Herbert pushed the huge cart away Ada gave me a bunch of bananas, a cabbage and a cucumber saying, "GIVE THESE TO YA MAM." I forced the bananas into one of my side coat pockets, the cucumber into the other, and held the cabbage under my

165

arm. As Herbert disappeared to some lock up with the cart Ada tipped the tin bath of water and left it upside down by the roadside.

Herbert reappeared and Ada said, "COME ON PASSY WE'LL HAVE A DRINK INT 'BARLEYCORN'." "Am only fourteen," I said wistfully to Ada, to which she answered, "DON'T WORRY ABOUT IT YUL BE ALRIGHT WI ME." "You'll be alreight wi Ada," Herbert echoed and laughed, "Ee, ee, ee." So once again I didn't fancy arguing with Ada, and so all three of us trapped up town to the 'Barleycorn Hotel' on Cambridge Street.

The Barleycorn was a real eye opener for a fourteen year old in the fifties. The place was full of smoke, and also, I thought, full of strange people. Besides being full of dodgy looking spiv type characters, there were a couple of men obviously dressed in women's clothes, there were also a couple of women dressed in men's clothes, they had short back and side hair cuts. At the bar sitting on a tall stool was a peroxide blond in a leopard skin coat black skirt hitched up showing off her stocking tops, and around her ankle a gold chain.

As the three of us stood at the bar I thought we must have looked a bit odd. 'Big Ada' looked a bit like the MP for Liverpool at the time, Bessie Braddock, only wider and definately more menacing, by her side 'Little muscly Herbert', a three foot six dwarf, and last but not least me, a tall stringy 'Teddy Boy'. I was doing my best to look like Elvis, but probably failing badly due to the fact that I'd got a bunch of bananas sticking out of one coat pocket, a cucumber out of the other, and a cabbage under my arm, definitely not Elvis.

Ada ordered in her usual loud way, "THREE HALVES." The barman who was serving her said, nodding in my direction, "How old is he?" Ada got mad at this and repeated, "AH SAID, THREE FUCKING HALVES." The barman began pulling the three halves, then laughing out loud, pointed to 'Little Herbert' and said to Ada, "Ah thought he'd be avin a short." To this Ada replied, "ANOTHER CRACK LIKE THAT UN, THAL GET A GLASS IN THI FACE, AH HOPE THA THINKS THAT'S FUNNY." The barman took it no further and proceeded to complete Ada's order of three halves. As he placed the three halves the peroxide blond leaned over from the stool and said to me, "Do ya fancy a good time love?" I was dumb struck, before I could think of answering Ada bailed in and said, pointing a menacing finger at the blond, "DON'T YOU CHUFFIN START;" end of conversation.

"COME ON," said Ada, "WE'LL SIT ONT BACK." There was a bit of a scuffle when a bloke with a walking stick lifted up the dress of one of the blokes who was dressed as a woman. He lifted the dress from behind with his stick. The bloke in the dress feeling the sudden draught swung round, and grabbed the stick wielding bloke by the throat and began to push him back onto the bar. There was a sound of breaking glass, order was soon restored when Ada bellowed out, "PACK IT IN OR I'LL CHUFFIN START."

A moment or two later a smart looking bloke

entered the pub. He was wearing a check sports coat, trilby hat, collar and tie, and was puffing on a pipe. Ada said to me, out of the corner of her mouth, "EYE, EYE, OTHER FIRMS IN." "Other firm?" I queried. "ARGH OTHER FIRM," Ada replied. "MUSKERS." "Muskers?" I again queried, for 'Muskers' and 'other firm' gave me no clue whatsoever. Ada pursed her lips together rolled her eyes in an exaggerated way and snapped, "CHUFFIN ELL, EYE MUSKERS, OTHER FIRM, ROZERS." I was just about to question, "Rozers?" when Ada translated, "CHUFFIN COPPER." "Oh ah see," I said. 'Little Herbert' shook his head slowly, he wasn't impressed by my naivety. "How do you know that?" I asked Ada. "WELL HE'S SUPPOSED TO BE IN PLAIN CLOTHS SO NOBODY KNOWS HE'S A COPPER, BUT HE MIGHT AS WELL WEAR A CARD ROUND HIS NECK SAYING 'COPPER'. JUST LOOK AT HIS PLATES," said Ada. She quickly translated, "PLATES OF MEAT, FEET, GERRIT." She didn't fancy going on with our question and answer scenario. "HE'S WEARING ALL HIS GOING OUT GEAR EXCEPT HIS STANDARD ISSUE POLICE BOOTS." The policeman ordered a half and stood at one end of the bar. "WATCH NAH PASSY AND THA'LL LEARN SUMMAT. MOST PEOPLE IN HERE ARE UP TO NO GOOD, AN HE'S NO DIFFERENT," Ada then went on to explain. "HE'LL FINISH HIS BEER SOON, AND THEN YA SEE HER AT OTHER END OF THE BAR, WELL SHE'S ON THE BATTER." I was just going to query 'batter' when Ada added, "A BRASS, ONT GAME, A PROSTITUTE."

The three of us sat staring at the situation. The

copper finished his half and slowly approached the peroxide blond in the leopard skin coat. Ada dug me in the ribs with her elbow to indicate her prediction was about to be proved correct. As the couple were leaving Ada shouted out sarcastically, "HAVE A GOOD TIME." The copper gave Ada a frowning stare. Then as he and his newly acquired partner left the pub Ada chimed up, "THAT'S WHAT YA CALL HELPING THE POLICE WITH THEIR ENQUIRES." The two blokes dressed like women started laughing. I made my excuses and then made my way home with Ada's words, "GIVE MY REGARDS TO YA DAD," ringing in my ears.

"Where've you been?" my mother asked as I walked into the house. "Ho just down town," I said, "Look what I've got you." I went on putting the bananas, cabbage, and cucumber on the table. "Oh there alright," said my mother in obvious pleasure, "Where did you get them from?" she asked. "Big Ada's given them me." My dad, who was sat reading the paper, looked over his glasses and chimed up, "Keep away from 'Big Ada' shell have ya int 'Barleycorn' before yal no where you are. Thiz some reight chuffs in that boozer I don't use it mi sen." I gulped and nodded in agreement.

For all of her hard exterior Ada had another side to her, I've been standing with her when she has shown tremendous acts of spontaneous kindness. One day an old bedraggled lady was making her way up Dixon Lane, Ada called her over, and filled a carrier bag full of all sorts of fruit and veg. 'Little Herbert' would volunteer to carry the old ladies bags to the nearest tram stop.

"THA SEES HER PASSEY" exclamed Ada, referring to the old lady, "LOST HER LAD INT WARS, WHATS GOVERNMENT DO FO HER, AL TELL THI SHALLA, SHITES MAGREG, CHUFF ALL", "WIV WON TWO WORLD WARS, AND OWD UNS O LEFT WITH A PITANCE".

On another day Ada remarked, "LOOK AT OLD HARRY, POOR SOD, LOST HIS WIFE LAST WEEK," she then said to 'Little Herbert', "ERE GIVE HARRY THIS 'HALF A BAR'." (Ten bob note). Herbert ran across to him and shoved it into the man's pocket; the recipient touched his cap in appreciation. Ada called over, "HAVE YOURSELF A DRINK, AN KEEP YA CHIN UP."

'Big Ada' and 'Little Herbert' were two great characters of Sheffield. 'Big Ada' was a sort of female 'Desperate Dan' figure. She could be loud, aggressive and sometimes outrageous, but to me, her good side outshone any detrimental characteristics by far. As for 'Little Herbert' he would be first in the queue to help people, yes two great characters who are sadly missed.

I once went into the 'Rag and Tag' market and there was a bloke selling black liquid in a bottle. He was shouting out his spiel saying, "This liquid will cure baldness, make you grow, cure piles, arthritis, and every other ailment." "Why don't we buy some dad?" I asked, to which my dad replied, "Cuz you'd end up with hairy piles." "What's piles?" I retorted. My dad's answer was simple, "Yu'll know if ya get em."

Another stallholder my dad knew was a bloke called Wilf who sold underwear and ladies and gents stockings. The ladies stockings sometimes had a photo of a film star in them; I remember Errol Flynn, Spencer Tracy and Betty Grable among others. Old Wilf used to get the ladies laughing as he shouted out, "All ladies knickers down today, if thi not down today thil be down toneet."

As a little kid and a teenager the market area was a magical place, a hive of activity and full of great characters, a working class shopping centre. To me all the market traders were sort of working class heroes, grafters one and all. They had to sell their goods every day to make a living.

Chapter 17

Match day

The highlight of any week for me as a teenager was Saturdays when Wednesday was playing at Hillsborough. Living off Neepsend Lane made getting to Hillsborough a bit easier than when at Martin Street, as Neepsend Lane was a direct route to the Wednesday ground. The entrance fee at the match was, if I remember correctly, nine pence (three and three-quarter new pence), and the tram fare was a penny (less than half a new pence) each way. So if you took four empty pop bottles back to the local shops the total refundable value would be a bob (five new pence) and with a bob in your pocket you were set up for the match.

I was always early I just couldn't wait to get in to Hillsborough. They opened the turnstiles at about 1:30pm for a 2:30pm kick-off. I was second in the queue one day when I noticed something that would mean more often than not, I would get into the match for free. The door to the turnstile ran on runners, so the bloke working the turnstile slid the door open, to start accepting customers. This particular day the door would not open fully, due to a bit of muck that was in the door channel. With the door partially open the bloke manning the turnstile called out to the lad at the front of the queue, "Scrape that channel for me son and I'll let you in for free." The lad scraped about a bit and sure enough bingo the door opened fully. The word 'free' hit me at once, and what had happened meant I would, nine times out of ten, get into the match for nowt.

So armed with a bob I would be off to Hillsborough. I would wait at the tram stop for the tram that would take me to Hillsborough. As the tram approached I would look to see the position of the conductor. His whereabouts was essential to my scheme as you will see. If the conductor was upstairs I would go downstairs, or visa versa. It was important that I kept as far from him as I could. I'd take my seat and the tram would chug along to Hillsborough. Hillsborough was about half a dozen stops away. When the conductor finally got round to me I would be, at most, only a couple of stops from the ground. He would reach me with the question, "Fares please?" to which I would hold out my fare (a penny) with the plaintive words, "One to town please." The conductor would be taken aback with this and reply, "Oh no son, you're going the wrong way." He'd say, "Come on," and walk me to the back of the tram for me to get off. He'd wave away my penny, which I was still offering, with the instructions, "Get off here, cross the road and get on the next tram going the other way, that will get you to town." He would follow this with a cautionary, "Careful as you go now."

With the first part of the mission complete there was a hundred yards walk to Hillsborough to be first in the queue. I would drop a penny in the channel of the turnstile to make sure the turnstile door would not fully open. Then sure enough, come opening time I would hear, "Scrape

174

channel free lad an al let thee in fo nowt." Little did he know that the only obstruction to the door fully opening was my penny, or my tram fare. I would pick up my penny and call out, "Try it nar, it should be o reight." He would slide the door fully open and say, "Come on ger ort top." Over the turnstile I would clamber and into the ground.

I did not mind the ground being deserted; I would gladly stand and stare at the football pitch. I would relive my memories of games that I had seen, and also look forward to the game I was about to see with great anticipation. I would stand behind the goal at the kop end, waiting for the action to start.

After the game I would be round to the player's entrance with my autograph book in my hand to get signatures of Wednesday players or whoever they were playing. My favourite Wednesday player was Derek Dooley. He burst on the scene to smash forty seven goals in one season only for the tragedy to strike the following year at Preston. Derek broke his leg and complications meant he had his leg amputated; tragically ending what would have been a fabulous career. Derek Dooley was simply irreplaceable. I recently bought a copy of Steven Farnsworth's book 'Dooley'. I went down to Bramall Lane to meet Derek and he kindly signed my book for me. At sixty odd years old I was still in awe of Derek for what he achieved as a player, manager, and administrator involved with both Wednesday and United. He should be known as 'Mr. Sheffield', a hero if ever there was one.

As an autograph hunter I met and spoke to all the

famous players of the fifties such as Stanley Matthews, Tom Finney, Billy Wright, the list is endless. Derek Dooley's testimonial at Hillsborough attracted all the great players to play and pay homage to Derek. I stood outside the player's entrance getting all the autographs. The last bloke to appear was the legendary Tommy Lawton. Tommy with his sleek jet black hair stood looking down at me. I was like a rabbit in the headlights of a car, I just looked up at him in amazement, and he eventually wandered off with a puzzled look on his face. I stood rigid, I was so in awe of him that I could not summon up the words, "Can I have your autograph please?"

Forty years later I did a drawing of Tommy. I contacted the Nottingham Evening Post to find Tommy's whereabouts. They very kindly put me in touch with Tommy who was in a nursing home. I sent my drawing to Tommy who very kindly signed it and returned it to me. Sadly Tommy died a few years ago.

I called at Hillsborough when Wednesday were in the premiership; I went to buy tickets for someone for a forthcoming game. Arsenal had just arrived; I could not believe there were barriers erected to keep the fans away from the players. Some Arsenal players signed autographs, but the barriers kept the fans away from touching distance. The working class game has been taken away from the working class. One of my dad's workmates at the Hallamshire Steel and File was Tommy Hoyland. His son Tommy was a regular player for Sheffield United and young Tommy would spend the closed season working at the same rolling mill. Oh how times have changed.

The other match day that I looked forward to even more was that of Hillfoot School games. If there was anything better than watching football, it was playing for Hillfoot School, a tremendous honour. My form teacher in 1956 was a Mr. Dowson. Mr. Dowson called me over one day and informed me that he would be in charge of the football team, adding that he knew nothing about football, but would do his best. He went on to suggest we should have a selection committee comprising of himself, me and another lad. He then asked if I knew any other lad who would be helpful in picking a team. Straight away I said, "Jack Fowler." Mr. Dowson questioned my nomination by saying, "Fowlers two years younger than you isn't he?" I agreed, but went on to tell him what a good player he was and not only that; he would also be the perfect captain.

So the three of us had our meeting, at which Jack declared, "I'll be captain." To this Mr. Dowson answered, "Your a bit sure of yourself aren't you Fowler?" I interrupted, "That's the reason he should be captain." Jack was a well built lad for his age. He stood out for three reasons, he had crew cut ginger hair, he was a tremendous footballer, and he was full of confidence. I knew losing would not be an option with Jack as captain.

Mr. Dowson then decided we would check out the football kit which was kept in a big wicker basket. Between us we pulled out the shirts, they were red with white sleeves. They were in a terrible state, torn, and the arms of the shirts were hanging off. They really were in a dilapidated state. Jack declared, "We could do with a new kit," to which Mr. Dowson quickly retorted, "Out of the question." So we came to the conclusion, or should I say Mr. Dowson came to the conclusion that each player would be allocated a shirt to take home for their respective mother's to wash and repair. I then dug deep into the kit basket and pulled out a leather football, if you could call it that.

It was deflated and sporting half a dozen tears in it, it looked more ready for cremation rather than football. I announced, "We can't play with this, it's had it." Mr. Dowson said, "Leave it with me I'll have a think," adding, "Is there anything else." Jack blurted out, "A bag for the ball and half a dozen oranges on match days for the players to suck at half time." The meeting was concluded with Mr. Dowson's words, "Leave it with me."

Mr. Dowson was a portly looking dark haired bespectacled bloke, not at all athletic looking, who spoke with a husky voice. But, nevertheless, I appreciated the fact that he would be in charge of the football team when he could have been doing other things that were more to his liking. So to Jack and I, Mr. Dowson was 'a good un'.

The next day in class, Mr. Dowson proclaimed that he'd given a lot of thought to our request for oranges, a bag for the ball, and indeed the ball. He queried, "Does anyone know were we can acquire a bag for the football, and oranges?" Straight away an arm shot up, it was a classmate Lenny Askham. "I'll get ya both," Lenny said adding, "Fo two bob." Mr. Dowson gave Lenny the two bob (ten pence) with the instructions that Friday was the deadline day, as it was a match day. "As for the ball," Mr. Dowson went on, "I think it could be repaired at the cobblers at a cost of about a shilling (five pence). He then said, holding out the lump of leather, "Off you go Pass, better take it now so we'll have it for Friday." He gave me the shilling and off on Penistone Road to the cobblers I went.

I had heard stories of the cobbler, so it was with some trepidation that I entered the shop. The cobbler was sitting bent over, working away at a shoe. He was a dark haired bloke who seemed to have a permanent fed up look to his face. This was probably due to the mountain of shoes, horse collars and bridles that surrounded him.

He spoke without looking at me, "What's tha want?" "Er, er, ave brought this ball to be mended." He carried on working, mumbling something under his breath. He finally stopped working, holding his arm out said, "Gee it ear," he then went on and on, beginning with a question, "Tha't from Hillfoot School arnt tha?" He didn't wait for confirmation but went on with the ball in his hand, "Tha sees this dunt tha? It's not a chuffin ball, it might av been one at one time a day, but it's not one nah." "Duz tha know how long ave been repairin this? Duz tha? Duz tha?" Before I could answer he went on, "Well al tell thi shala? Since 1940, it's not a cobbler tha wants it's a chuffin magician."

My heart sank. I managed to stammer out, "Teacher sez it only needs a few stitches." "A few stitches," he explodes, "A few chuffin stitches, and it's got more stitches than Al Capone. Tha noze if this warra horse it ave been shot years aggu. In fact it looks as if it needs a blood transfusion, a don't know abhart stitches. In fact it looks as if it needs anaesthetic, a dunt no what teachers doin sendin ya on errands like this."

It went deathly silent while he looked down at the patient. The silence was broken by him saying, "Ah must be bloody daft." I was relieved, it sounded as though he was going to have a go repairing our ball. He then said, "How much av thi sent fot job?" I meekly answered, "A shilling." This caused another eruption, "A shillin, a chuffin shillin. Tha noze if that teacher o yors wo buildin pyramids thid oney ave cost fifty bob (two pounds and fifty new pence). A chuffin shillin, ave never nown owt like it." He concluded by saying, "Geerz thi bob, thal afta leervit wi mi."

I had to interrupt by saying, "We need it by Friday." "Friday," he exploded, "Tha must be jokin, tha sees this lot," cocking his thumb over his shoulder at the mountain of shoes, "That's all work," and going on with a question, "An I'm supposed to leaerve that lot to repair your ball forra bob?" He concluded, "Thal av to keep thi fingers crossed, that's all ah ken sey, burra can't see it, not in a hundred chuffin years."

Come Friday morning in class Mr. Dowson asked, "Askham did you manage to get a bag for our football, and oranges for half time refreshment?" "Yes sir," Askham replied. He approached our teacher's desk putting out an onion bag and three large cooking apples. "What's these?" Mr. Dowson asked referring to the cooking apples. "Thid not got no oranges so I got next best thing." Frowning Mr. Dowson called out, "Will these do Pass?" To which I replied, "Yes sir." I did not want to put a downer on Lenny's scam. It was obvious he'd been to Mrs. Kenworthy's fruit shop, and knowing Mrs. Kenworthy, he would have got both bag and apples for nowt. While I was sitting I just could not imagine Stanley Mathews chomping on a cooking apple at half time.

"Off you go Pass," said Mr. Dowson interrupting my imagination, "Go and get our ball from the cobblers." On entering the cobblers I feared the worst. The cobbler once again did not look up but carried on with his work. I must have stood a full five minutes in total silence. It seemed an absolute age. He finally responded by bending under the counter to produce our ball. "Ere," he said holding out the ball. I snatched it with glee, "Thanks mister."

"All it wants now," said the cobbler, "is some 'Dubbin' on it, ah don't suppose yuv gorrany at school av ya?" I shook my head. The cobbler then chucked me a huge tin of 'Dubbin' saying, "Ear cop fo this." I was full of smiles and thanks when the cobbler interrupted, "Just do us a favour will tha? Tell your teacher when horsez deerd, its chuffin deerd." On my way back to school I looked down at the tin of 'Dubbin', the price on the tin was a shilling, so for all of his brusque manor he repaired our ball for nothing. The cobbler was as good as gold.

On returning to class I passed on the message to the teacher, "Cobbler sez whent horsez deerd, its deerd."

Mr. Dowson looked puzzled and obviously did not get the message, for on seeing the tin of 'Dubbin' he said, "Oh that was good of him, we'll have to go back next year." And I thought, "Not Chuffin likely."

We got the season off with a bang, beating Sacred Hearts 9-3; we even got a mention in the Saturday sports paper the Green-un. The mini headline was '3 hat tricks sink Sacred Hearts', and went on to say 'an impressive performance by Hillfoot school saw off much fancied Sacred Hearts, in beating them 9-3. Three Hillfoot lads each got a hat trick, the goals for Hillfoot were scored by Pass, Ward and Toothill.' We seemed to go from strength to strength, winning with such margins as 10-1, 9-0, and 7-1. In games such as 10-1, after the game our captain Jack Fowler would go on and on about the one goal we had conceded. Further proof, if proof was necessary, that he was the perfect choice of captain.

We were competing for the United Shield, and we reached the semi-finals winning twelve games, including friendlies, twelve wins and no draws or defeats. In the semi-final we had drawn Carbrook School who had a reputation of being a good side. As the game was played on their ground it was custom that the visiting team manager would ref the game, in our case, Mr. Dowson.

Before the game Mr. Dowson went to great lengths to explain that he knew very little about the rules of football, but that nevertheless he would ref the game to the best of his ability. We got off to a great start and I scored early on. But disaster was about to strike, the rules of the game state that you can't be offside when receiving the ball from a throw in. We were awarded a throw in, Jack Fowler threw the ball to me, to which Mr. Dowson blew his whistle and called out, "Offside Pass."

In a flash Jack Fowler protested, "Ya can't be offside from a throw in." Mr. Dowson retorted, "Get on with the game Fowler. I told you before hand I knew little of the rules of football." Jack answered by saying, "Tha shunt av whistle in thee hand if tha noze nowt abhart fuckin job." Mr. Dowson was furious of Jack's choice of words. He sent Jack off with the comment, "I'll not have language like that."

Just before half time Carbrook scored to make it 1-1, and just after half time took the lead 2-1. We with ten men were up against it. Every time I was anywhere near Mr. Dowson I would chip away at him saying, "We'll not win without Fowler." I said this over and over again until about fifteen minutes from time Mr. Dowson called out, "I think you've learnt your lesson Fowler, you may come back on."

Pandemonium broke out from Carbrook's teacher and supporters quite rightly saying, "You can't send some one off then bring them back on." To make matters worse, or should I say better, Jack on returning to the game was inspired to score a hat trick to leave us comfortable winners 4-2. We were through to the final. A big argument arose from Mr. Dowson's decision to bring Jack back on the field of play. As we got on our bus, there were shouts of, "You won't get away with it," and all sorts of protestations.

A few days later our headmaster Mr. Simmons entered our classroom and said to Mr. Dowson, "Could you pop into my office at lunchtime?" and added, "Bring Pass along with you." As Mr. Dowson and me entered the heads office Fowler was already there. The head started off by saying, "We have had a strong protest from Carbrook School's teachers, regarding our 4-2 victory over their school in the semi-final. They say one of our boys was sent off, and then brought back on to play a major part in our victory." "That's correct," said Mr. Dowson.

Mr. Simmons said, "Let me tell you my interpretation of the events as I see it. In a highly charged game of such importance Fowler in his keenness spoke out of turn, and you Mr. Dowson quite rightly sent him off. Then when you saw he had quietened down you quite rightly brought him back on." I thought, "Chuffin ell he's not only asking questions, but he's answering them an all."

"I have come to the conclusion that you refereed the game with commonsense," said Mr. Simmons. "I think it's just a case of sour grapes from the Carbrook people." He then went on to say he would sort the matter out with the head teacher of Carbrook and let us know the result. He sent us on our way with, "Oh by the way congratulations on such a fine win."

Nothing came of Carbrook's protestations; we were through to the final. We would be playing at the Owlerton dog track. As we had already beaten Morley Street 7-1 earlier in the season we were confident of winning the final. Alas, it was not to be, we never performed well on the day. Morley Street won 2-1. We were devastated, but nevertheless Morley Street deserved to win on the day. I suppose that's why football is such a great game, nothing is a foregone conclusion.

No mention of football and Hillfoot School would be complete without mentioning the 1981 F.A. Cup Final at Wembley between Spurs and Manchester City. I had no allegiance to either team. The significance of the occasion to me was the fact that the referee in charge of the showpiece of the Football Association calendar was Keith Hackett, ex Hillfoot School pupil. I felt like cheering as he walked out at Wembley. Keith a working class lad from Parkwood Springs was at the pinnacle of his career as a ref.

As you will have gathered I am and will always be football daft. I played football, ran football teams, and even refereed (Gulp). Although biased, in my opinion Keith was the finest referee this country ever produced.

Keith went all over the world, and I'm sure in doing so, enhanced the reputation of English referees every where he went. Keith's strong points were that he had commonsense in abundance; and also something that is a gift, tremendous presence.

Keith also refereed Sunday morning games in local Sheffield parks. In my opinion it was sometimes a greater test, what with no linesmen, no sort of protection, and three or four hundred locals all putting the ref. under pressure that was to Keith, a piece of cake.

Keith is now supremo in charge of all Premiership refs. It could not have gone to a better man.

Whenever they were in the same division the biggest league games were, without a doubt, 'Wednesday' against 'United'. I can remember all the 'Wednesday' victories as if they were yesterday, but somehow, I can't remember much about the games when 'United' won. I suppose it's only natural with me being a 'Wednesdayite'.

I don't really enjoy derby games I'm probably too full of apprehension. I feel its like going to the dentist, you have to go, but you're glad when its all aver. When 'United' win you have to put up with all of the banter from the 'Unitedites', and when 'Wednesday' win the 'Unitedites' have to put up with the banter from 'Wednesdayites', it's the same problem.

I once went to Anfield to watch a game between Liverpool at home to Manchester United. The behaviour of some of the 'fans' from both sets of supporters was to put it mildly appalling. Some of the Liverpool 'fans' sang derogatory songs about the Munich air disaster, and in return some Manchester United 'fans' sang songs about the death of the late great Bill Shankly. Both sets of 'fans' that were involved were in the minority but nevertheless could be heard loud and clear, but for me, it spoiled the whole occasion.

The games between 'Wednesday' and 'United' create plenty of banter, but that's all it is, banter. I will go on to prove the point.

Perhaps the biggest ever Derby game between the

two Sheffield clubs was on the third of April 1991 at Wembley in the semi-final of the F.A. Cup. As kick-off approached the 'United' manager, who at that time was, Dave Bassett was walking around the perimeter of the pitch to take up his position to watch the game. Usually whichever manager it was would get some ribbing from the opposing fans. On this particular day along side Dave was a young goalkeeper 'United' had signed from West Brom; he was a lad by the name of Mel Rees. Mel would be taking no part in the game as he was suffering from cancer. The poor lad looked gaunt, for the terrible disease was beginning to have an effect on his appearance. As the two approached a large contingent of 'Wednesday' fans my heart was in my mouth. I needn't have bothered. The 'Wednesdayites' broke out in spontaneous applause for the lad and began chanting "There's only one Mel Rees." Mel waved to the 'Wednesdayites' in appreciation. It was one of the most moving moments I have ever witnessed at a football match. The result seemed irrelevant after that. However, I must tell you 'Wednesday' won 2 – 1 after extra time. In fact bar for 'United's' goalkeeper, Alan Kelly, it would have and should have been 10 – 1. (Its only banter 'Unitedites').

To redress the balance 'United' a few years later came to Hillsbrough to play 'Wednesday'. Two 'Wednesday' fans had been killed in a road accident going to a previous away game. A two minutes silence was held in respect of the two fans, which was impeccably adhered to by all the 'United' fans. As for the result of that game, I just can't remember.

To take it a stage further, a couple of years ago, I attended the funeral of a 'Wednesday' player of the forties and fifties, Vin Kenny. I had spent lots of time in his company at the Owlerton greyhound track. In attendance that day was ex 'United' player Tommy Hoyland. I thought it tremendous that an ex 'United' player should pay his respects to an ex 'Wednesday' player. In reality it should not have been a surprise, anyone knowing Tommy would know it to be typical of the man.

So for me Sheffield have without a doubt the two best sets of football fans in the country. Though I must add I think 'Wednesdayites' are just slightly better. (Banter.)

Chapter 18

A day at the City Hall

It was announced one day at school that there would be a trip to the City Hall to see John Barbirolli and his orchestra. As it was in school time 'Chappie' and I were certainly up for it. The trip was for our class only, and would take place on the forthcoming Friday. Our teacher reminded us to be on our best behaviour as the school head Mr. Simmons would be in charge. A total of forty boys were to attend the concert.

Come the Friday and Mr. Simmons warned us that we must never forget we would all be representing Hillfoot School. The coach arrived at the school gates, and we were all to enter the coach by the back door. Mr. Simmons told the driver, "Count them all on driver, we have a party of forty, I'm just going to my office for the necessary paperwork."

Tony and I were first on the coach and straight away opened the emergency door on the opposite side of the coach, then we began to usher all the kids that were getting on, to get straight back off and go back in the queue to get back on. The driver who was armed with a pencil and paper was getting a bit flustered with the never ending queue. He lifted off his flat cap and with the same hand started to scratch his head in puzzlement. Someone said, "Watchit Head teacher's comin." Quick as a flash

Tony and I closed the emergency door and took up our seats. We heard the driver call out to the head, "Arghmany did tha sey? Worrit forty? Well somatts up av got eighty nine on and thiz still this lot," pointing with his overworked pencil to the remnants of the queue. "Impossible driver," the head declared. "Just get them all on and we'll have a count up." Once everyone was on the head did his count, interrupted by a few, "Sit stills," he finally announced, "forty, yes just forty, driver let's be on our way."

When we got to the City Hall we were each handed a one sheet programme listing the works of music that were to be performed. The seats for our class were situated behind the orchestra and facing a packed auditorium of kids from all schools in Sheffield.

Once the music started everything before us was blacked out except for three beams of light illuminating the orchestra. Tony and I sat by the side of a lad from our class called John Clay. John handed out some chewing gum. John said, "It would be a laugh if we could make little balls of chewing gum and flick them at the brass section," which we immediately started to do. We flicked away merrily, occasionally hitting a bulls eye. When we did connect, it sent out a clear 'Ping'. Old John Barbirolli was mystified by the strange sounds coming from the brass section as he was conducting. He frowned at the brass section each time there was a 'Ping', they in turn reacted by raising their eyebrows in bewilderment.

When we had run out of chewing gum Tony had an idea. Tony was a wiz at making paper darts. So then we commandeered the programmes off about twenty or so of our classmates and passed them to Tony to get to work. Once completed Tony, John and I were suitably armed with handfuls of paper darts and ready for action. "Now," Tony said and we began to throw the paper darts as high as we could. They disappeared into the darkness and then came zig zagging through the shafts of lights, disappearing in the darkness, then finally back into the light, occasionally hitting the musicians. The audience, who we could not see, began laughing.

John Barbirolli called a halt to proceedings and stopped the music by tapping his baton on a music stand. All the lights went on in the City Hall; there was some confusion for a while. Then after a pause of about five minutes, the conductor tapped the music stand a couple of times, the lights went out and the music started up again.

The three of us were giggling thinking we had got away with it, and then something gripped my neck. "Argh," I exclaimed. Mr. Simmons whispered, "My office Monday morning Pass." Then he grabbed Tony, "Argh," with the same comment following, and then with the same to John Clay. As we left the City Hall we had comments from all the other kids, like, "Yorv ad it on Monday." We replied, as you do when you're scared of the consequences, "Wi not boverd."

'Chappie' and I were first on the coach and, as when we set off, the driver was doing his counting bit. This time I opened the emergency door and encouraged the kids to enter that way instead of joining the queue. Word went round, "Hey up Simmons is comin." So I closed the emergency door and sat down. "Come on Driver lets be on our way." The driver said, "We can't, wiv orny got twenty eight on board." Mr. Simmons replied, "Nonsense," jumped aboard, did his counting and ordered, "Back to Neepsend driver," and we were on our way back home.

On our way back Mr. Simmons declared, "Pass, Chapman, and Clay my office after assembly Monday morning. I'm quite looking forward to seeing the three of you."

Standing before Mr. Simmons was not what we were looking forward to. Nevertheless, there we were. "Your behaviour was appalling," said Mr. Simmons, "And you will be suitably punished." "Chapman," he blurted out, "You represent the school at swimming don't you?" "Yes sir," replied Tony. "And you Pass represent the school at football is that correct?" "Yes sir." "As for you Clay what do you represent the school at?" "Nowt sir." "One thing for certain," he went on, "you have all represented the school at messing about." All three of us started to smile, "Don't you dare smile as I'm addressing you." Our smiles faded away into a frown.

"I was going to stop your swimming and you your football and give you two strokes each; but as Clay does not represent the school at anything, and that any punishment must be equal, I'm giving each one of you four strokes of the cane." Bang, crash, wallop. It was all over in a couple of minutes and the three of us trudged back to the class room with numb hands. As for Tony and I, an extra two strokes was better than any exclusion from swimming and football.

On reflection the punishment was fully justified and did not change my high regard for Mr. Simmons or, in fact for all the teachers at Hillfoot School.

Chapter 19

Touché

In my final year at school I had a teacher who, although I didn't realise it at the time, took an interest in my writing. He would mark my compositions, essays now. He would use words I had never heard of. After one particular composition he wrote at the bottom in red ink, 'You are getting to be a hobbledehoy.' I was determined not to ask him what he meant by hobbledehoy, but set myself the task of trying to find out myself. I found the answer through a lady teacher who had a huge comprehensive dictionary. Hobbledehoy was, she informed me, "a raw, awkward young fellow, especially one between boyhood and manhood." So in my next composition I used the word hobbledehoy as though I knew the meaning. The teacher and I were fencing with words. He would always be the winner because he had the brains, but I was determined to parry his efforts. The composition that included the word hobbledehoy was marked up by him.

This time he wrote on the bottom in his customary red ink, 'Your work is both good and original, unfortunately the good work is not original, and the original part is not good.'

This baffled me a bit so I approached an unsuspecting cohort, the lady teacher, and repeated the comments. "Oh," she said straight away, "That's a quote from Samuel Johnson." "Who was Samuel Johnson?" I asked. "Oh," she went on, "He was a master of the English language; He produced among other things comprehensive dictionaries", and then added, "Your teacher is a big fan of his." Composition time came round again. This time my teacher singled me out saying, "You Pass write me something funny." "What about?" I queried. The non smiling teacher said, "What about? I am giving you freedom, and all you want is restrictions." He curtailed the conversion with the word, "Anything."

I wrote a composition about a fool. I cannot remember the content but the title of the composition was, 'Sam Johnson the Fool'. I watched as he marked my work, stone faced as usual. "Pass," he called out, handling my work sideways at arms length whilst his eyes were transfixed on the desk in front of him. I collected my composition and sat down. I couldn't wait to read his comments. At the bottom of the composition he wrote, 'From picking it up, to putting it down again I was engulfed in uncontrollable laughter at your composition.' Finally adding, 'One day I hope to find time to read it.'

He was always on about reading as well as writing. He used to say, "The written word was not always to be read in the obvious." To use an example he wrote on the blackboard the following question, 'Would a one armed man find it difficult to change an electric light bulb?' He looked at his watch and declared, "You have five minutes to think of an answer." He stared down at his watch for the full five minutes then announced, "Times up. How many think yes it could be difficult for a one armed man to change a light bulb." Unanimously the class voted yes. The teacher then declared the answer was, "No," explaining, "A one armed man would find it easy to change a light bulb provided he had kept his receipt."

One day he was telling us that, when writing, the situation you write about dictates, or should do, the way you write. For instance, if you have a man lost in the desert with water in a canteen you should write, 'His canteen is half empty'. Should the man not be lost, on getting back to civilisation his canteen should be described as, 'Still half full'. His point was half empty and half full is exactly the same, but the situation is different.

He had just finished this particular lesson when in burst our head teacher Mr. Simmons. In his hand was a first proof of the school magazine to which all classes contributed. He said he wanted a final footnote of just a few lines to finish off the magazine and asked for any volunteers, before anyone could answer our teacher said, "Pass will do it." "Well done Pass," the head declared, adding, "I'll be back in fifteen minutes."

After ten minutes or so our teacher queried, "Have you completed the task?" "I have," I replied and placed before him my footnote. It read, 'Someone has written on the school playground 'Half the teachers at Hillfoot School are daft', as a pupil I disagreed by saying half the teachers at Hillfoot School are not daft'. Straight faced he read my input, unsmiling he said, "Are you willing to face the consequences, if I give Mr. Simmons your contribution?" He meant I was risking getting the cane should the head realise what I'd written. "Yes," I said.

The head returned and was handed my footnote. My teacher looked straight ahead expressionless as the head read my notes. He then shook his head from side to side, when the head said, "Wonderful Pass, what a wonderful compliment to the teachers of Hillfoot School."

My final teacher never gave compliments but very cleverly aroused my interest in writing. He was a stickler for decorum and would get mad if you referred to him as sir. He would say, "I have not had the honour", pause then add, "Yet, to have received a knighthood. You refer to me as Mister and I refer to you as boy."

Years after leaving school I was in the fish market and I saw the teacher staring down with a frown on his face, looking at cockles, muscles and crabs and such. I could not resist approaching him, and due to his fondness for decorum I said, "Nah then me owd pal, ar ya doin?" He never looked up but asked, "Pass have you any knowledge about shellfish?" "No," I answered. He then asked if I had a job that involved writing. "No," I came back with, "Ah work in a scrap yard." He wandered off muttering, "Sounds just about right, just about right." He was a wonderful teacher whose name I'm not telling you.

We're still fencing.

Chapter 20

Starting work

In my final term at Hillfoot School we had loads of visitors from all sorts of prospective employers, police, railways, and building firms offering apprenticeships in bricklaying and plumbing. Every conceivable trade was represented. Their aim was to try to entice you to join their organisation. All you had to do was to pick a trade and off you went into the real world, as the teachers would say. I was often warned by teachers that if I did not make a greater effort I would end up sweeping the streets. I bet you need qualifications to sweep the streets nowadays (So don't say kids don't know they're born today).

One of my teachers told me he had contacted The Sheffield Star, and told them I could turn out to be a useful recruit for their newspaper. He told me my writing could eventually be put to good use working in the newspaper industry. I met these two blokes from 'The Star' who went through the procedure of working my way up from making tea, to reaching the ultimate goal, that of a reporter. I was told to discuss the issue with my parents, and if I was still interested to contact them. I had told 'The Star' representatives that I could not spell, they were not deterred by this saying the problem could be rectified. The job sounded a bit upmarket for me, and my dad agreed. He dismissed the offer with the comment,

"Dunt sound like a proper job to me," and that was an end to the matter.

My mother said that she had heard that there were jobs to be had at the nearby John Bedford's who made small tools such as spanners. She said they were looking for apprentice machine fitters. As the job was local it would be handy living within walking distance to work, therefore saving on any unnecessary extra costs of bus fares. So off I went to John Bedford's for an interview with the words, "Just answer any questions honestly," ringing in my ears.

I presented myself at the time house, and was soon directed to the office of firm's manager. A loud, "Come in," bellowed out from the office after I had hesitantly knocked. I faced the manager who, strangely to me, looked like a farmer. He was a big thick set bloke with a ruddy complexion and, I noticed, huge hands. Part of his clothing was a green cardigan, tie, checked shirt, and a sports jacket. He did not seem to fit in with the rest of the noisy surroundings.

The interview went like this:
Manger: "What can I do for yo mi lad?"
Me: "Ave come fo a job."
Manager: "Righto lets see then." He went on: "Which school do you come from?"
Me: "Hillfoot."
Manger: "Are you good at metal work?"
Me: "No."

Manager: "Woodwork then?"

Me: "No."

Manager: "Are you interested in machinery?"

Me: "No."

Manger: "The working of engines, cars and the like?"

Me: "No."

Manager: "Have you heard of our company's good name?"

Me: "No."

Manager: "Can you see yourself setting up machines?"

Me: "No."

Manager: O'right then, start on Monday, 8 o'clock, and don't be late.

I came away feeling quite pleased with myself. I'd exercised my mother's instructions to the letter and I'd got myself a job. (Kids don't know thi born today).

I proudly announced to my mother that I'd got the job. "Oh you have done well," she said. Then she asked, "How much are you going to be paid?" It had never crossed my mind to ask about wages. "Never mind," she said, "Al go intut market and get you some overalls and working boots."

Later that evening my mother said to me, "Try these overalls on, they might want taking up a bit." "Up a bit," was an understatement; these thick dark blue overalls were so big that I could get in and out of them without undoing the buttons. My mother did the necessary alterations then announced holding up the overalls, "Nah then, that's better, try em on now." I tried them on; I'd got seven inch turn ups on the sleeves and seven inch turn ups on the trouser legs. The arse of the overalls was in line with my knee caps, and the sleeves were so long, if I stood with my hands by my side, you could only see the tips of my fingers. "Ah ya look smashing," said my mother. "You'll grow into um. There a pair of really serviceable overalls is them."

I hated the words serviceable, for when my mother said it; roughly translated it meant they would last for ever. I'd had two previous encounters with the word serviceable the first time was with a snake belt, bought for me at the age of seven. I still had it at the age of fifteen. The other time was with Wellington boots; I had the same pair that had previously been our Brian's from the age of seven to the age of about twelve. "Come on," my mother encouraged me, "Try ya boots on." "Thi too big," I said. "No," contradicted my mother, "Yul grow into em."

I winced as she said, "A good serviceable pair of boots." I looked in the mirror and held my arms out by my side. There was no daylight showing under the arms. The overalls were that big I could not stop myself from thinking, "I look like a giant fruit bat." The boots being a size too big, made me feel like a deep sea diver. I had to make a deliberate effort just to get them off the ground. I didn't have to make an effort to put them back down. They felt so heavy gravity did it for me, hitting the floor with a great big clump.

My first workmate Harry Marriott, a good lad,
pursuing his hobby of bottle collecting

Although John Bedford's was close by I allowed myself half an hour to get me there, due to the overall and boots. My mother wished me luck as I set off with the words, "Ask em what wages are." The legs of the overalls sort of rustled as I walked and due to the boots I was wearing I took long strides.

So off I went with a rustle – clump – rustle. I knocked on the manager's office door, no answer, only this time a lad of about my age opened the door to ask, "First day?" "Yes," I replied. "Come on in," he said. "My name's Harry." Harry was a good looking lad and was most welcoming. "Sit ya self darn," he said pointing to a leather clad swivel chair. The chair was behind a huge desk which was by the side of a roaring fire. On the fire was a huge kettle that was permanently boiling, as I sat myself down Harry said, "Fancy a cup o tea?" "Argh go on then," I replied. Harry made me a big pot of tea then asked, "Fancy a slice a toast?" "Go on then," I said thinking if this is work give me more. Harry cut me a slice of bread then passed it to me with a large toasting fork. So I'm sat hunched up toasting this bread, when Harry passes me a cig with the words, "Ere have a smoke."

I'm sitting in this posh leather chair toasting bread with a cig dangling from my lips, when the door to the office opens and in walks the works manager. "What the chuffin ell?" he declares, and then goes on, "Sat in my chair, smoking, toasting my bread, and drinking my tea. You cheeky little bugger," he went on, "I hope this is not going to be typical. Ya first day an ya just sat lounging abarht. Ya here to work young man, in all my years' ave seen nowt like it. What ya got to say fo yuself, come on?" he demanded. Remembering my mother's last words I stood up and said, "What's wages?" To this he exploded, "What's wages? What's wages? Ya cheeky chuff, yul be lucky to last week arght. Thiz just you two starting today. He seems OK." He said indicating to Harry, "But as for you, I can't see you lasting a week." Harry had set me up but there was no way I was going to tell this to the works manager I would have to bide my time and get my own back.

We were taken to the spanner department and introduced to the spanner department foreman. "You go down to the bottom end machine," he said, "Ask for Jim Benson." Harry was put with some other machinist. "Are you Mr. Benson?" I enquired, to which this dark haired bespectacled bloke replied, "Oh, yes, just call me Jim. Ya first day?" He questioned. I nodded. "Well I'm a surface grinder," he said adding, "Yul soon pick it up. Ah tell ya what," he went on, "Gu tut file department and tell em you come fo a long rest, tell em Jim's sent ya." He pointed to a door close by and off I went. I crossed a sort of cobbled courtyard and asked directions from a fellow worker and ended up in a huge hanger type building full of people on small drop hammers working like mad.

"What ya want?" This big vest wearing bloke asked, I nervously replied, "Ave come fo a long rest." "OK," replies the bloke, "Just stay where you are," then disappears into the darkness.

I was standing there for what seemed like an age, when out

of nowhere up pops the works manager, "What the bleedin ell o ya doin here ya supposed to be int spanner department?" To which I replied, "Ave come for a long rest." The manager comes back with "How long have you been stood there?" I came back with, "About an hour," to which he says, "Well yuv had one, get back to spanner department."

I walked back into the spanner department to loud applause from the about thirty or so that worked there. Harry was walking past and said, "Fancy falling for that." "Where ya goin?" I asked him. "Oh I'm fetching a bag of sparks for my mate," he replied whilst disappearing through the doorway.

The wages turned out to be £2-2s-0d a week (Two pounds and ten pence in today's money) plus a free dinner token each day. The wages could be renegotiated once you reached the age of eighteen. The dinner tokens were a bit of a laugh, they had to be queued for at dinnertime, by the time you got your token you had to have what was left. Sometimes it would be fried egg and mashed potatoes. Sometimes two slices of beef and fish. I handed my weekly wage packet over to my mother and in return I'd get back ten shillings spending money (fifty pence).

The job was mind blowingly boring. Jim would get a set of spanners up on a sort of moving magnet bed, set the machine going for about half an hour. Then repeat the process. After about six months I moved on to help a bloke called Jack Rawson who operated a milling machine, this was equally as boring.

Despite his antics I found I got on really well with Harry, who like me was a Wednesdayite. Harry hailed from a district in Sheffield called Woodthorpe, which Harry pronounced, "Woodforp." As a bit of a bonus, Harry and I could work over Saturday mornings 8am while 12 for which we each received an extra ten bob (fifty pence).

On one particular Friday we agreed to work the following morning. The spanner shop foreman gave us our instructions. The spanner department had two lines of about twelve machines with an aisle down the centre. At one end was a huge skip of 'to be worked on' spanners. We had to load these spanners into tray like tins, 12 dozen to each tin. Load the tins onto a barrow that jacked up. We had then to proceed down the line placing the tins by the side of each machine. Harry doing one side me the other, each one giving the other one a lift with the heavy tins. The most important thing was to make sure there were exactly 12 dozen in each tin. The machinists were on piece work and it was important to them that the numbers were right for filling in their work sheets. So as we were starting work this particular Saturday morning Harry asked me how many is 12 dozen, quick as a flash I reply 132. Off we went chatting away about all sorts of subjects whilst working.

Halfway through the morning on the following Monday, all hell was let loose; all sorts of arguing going on, you could say there was a spanner in the works. It all resulted in the appearance of the works manager who demanded, "You two in my office." Once Harry and I were in the office the works manager asked Harry, "Which side machines were you supplying right or left?" "Can't remember," said Harry quickly going on the defensive. "OK," said the works manager, "I'll give you each a test. Write down the number of 12 dozen," giving us both a slip of paper and a pencil. We both handed in our answers and to me he said, "You go back to work."

As I left his office I could hear him saying to Harry, "Do you realise the trouble you have caused? What school did you go to?" and so on. After Harry's tea, toast and make yourself at home caper I'd got my own back. We both stayed at John Bedford's for one year. Harry had heard of jobs going as van lads at Yorkshire Egg Producers on City Road. The wages were exactly double of what we were earning, £4-4s-0d a week (four pounds and twenty pence). But that's another story.

An interesting fact was that out of my first week's wages my dad gave me a pound note back, he said, "Frame it as the first pound you ever earnt." I bought a frame from Woolworths for sixpence (two and a half pence) and framed it. Years and years later I came across it whilst rummaging through a drawer, and do you know what the spending power of the pound was? It was an old sixpence, because at that time the cost of frames was a pound.

Fall out from "Weerz me Dad?"

Through writing "Weerz me Dad?" I was contacted by Wendy Thompson. Wendy had done work on my family tree. Due to Wendy's diligence I found out that my mother's dad, James Thomas Stones, had been adopted aged four. A fact that I never was aware of I'm sure my late mother did not know this for I'm sure she would have mentioned it. Through Wendy I was contacted by Mrs. Kathy Thacyk of Saskatchewan, Canada, who had been compiling information about her maiden name Pass. It has not been concluded yet but there is a possibility that we could be related. Small world, hang on it's about to get smaller.

I was awoken one morning about 4 o'clock, my phone was ringing. I answered, "Yes." The bloke at the other end of the phone call introduced himself as John Lee. He went on to say that he'd read "Weerz me Dad?" and was complimentary about it. I thanked him for his comments but pointed out that it was a strange time in the morning to be having such a conversation. He apologised by saying he had, "forgot the time difference." "Time difference?" I queried. "I'm phoning from Australia," he went on to say that he'd left Sheffield in the late fifties. He said that he was still familiar with areas of Sheffield because he re-visits from time to time.

He then enquired about what district I lived in. When I answered "Wisewood," he was quite amazed. "I suppose you have a Post Office called Wisewood Post

Office, my local Post Office here in Australia is called Wisewood Post Office." I asked him if I could guess where in Australia he was phoning from. He said I could but Australia being such a big country he could not imagine I'd get it right. When I told him that my guess was that he was phoning from Ferntree Gully, he was gob smacked. "Wow," he declared, "How did you come to that conclusion?"

I went on to say that my cousin had left England for Australia in 1959, and the last time that she wrote she pointed out that she was working in a Post Office, in fact the Wisewood Post Office, Ferntree Gully. He couldn't believe his ears; he queried, "They don't call her Margaret do they?" When I said they did he could not believe it and answered, "I was talking to Margaret less than an hour ago!" Small World init?

The kindness of people never ceases to amaze me. I had a call from Mrs. Christine Mason. She phoned to say she had read the book "Weerz me Dad?" She said she was really moved by the death of Peter Marshall at such a young age.

She went on to say that she hoped I didn't mind but she had gone to great lengths and all sorts of trouble searching through Sheffield Archives. Through her efforts she had tracked down Peter's final resting place in Burngreave Cemetery. The fact that Peter's grave was unmarked by stone or cross made her efforts really difficult.

My wife and I met up with Christine at Burngreave Cemetery and planted some flowers on Peter's unmarked plot. Thanks Christine.

I will relay this funny story regarding "Weerz me Dad?" The scene: I was sitting at a large table at W.H. Smiths, Meadowhall. I was signing copies of "Weerz me Dad?" The kind people of W.H. Smiths had supplied me with tea and biscuits.

As I was sipping my tea two old ladies approached the table. They both looked to be in there seventies. They were hooked together arm-in-arm, one had a hearing aid in her left ear, the other in her right ear. One had a stick in her left hand, the other in her right hand. They looked perfect, they could have been sisters. They had the perfect solution to their disabilities. Between them they had two good legs and two good ears. They approached my table suspiciously.

One of the old ladies picked up a copy of "Weerz me Dad?" Then she said to the other, "Shall we have one?" The other old lady answered with an, "Eh?" The first old lady snapped back, repeating the question, to which the second old lady mildly replied, "Ah suppose so."

I began to sign my book only to be interrupted by the first old lady, "Oui, stop that, ah don't want one wi scribblin init." Probably feeling a little bit important I smiled and said, "I'm not scribbling, I'm the author." To which the second old lady demanded, "What's eh sey?" The leader of the duo translated, "Eh sez thi call im Arthur. A don't know what difference that makes." Going on to demand one with no writing in the old lady offered me payment for the book. I directed them to the pay desk.

Due to their deafness they caused quite a stir and people gathered round all laughing at my predicament.

Once at the pay desk one of the old ladies said to the girl behind the counter, "Ah sey love yul not sell many books, that blokes scribbling inum." The girl replied, "He's the author, he's signing copies." "What's shi sey?" asked the second old lady once more. "She sez same as him, they call im Arthur, worlds gone chuffin mad, come on."

Before leaving the shop they stopped briefly at my table. The old lady in charge bent her head down in my direction and said, "Daft chuff", and then drifted out into Medowhall.

"Weerz me Dad?" was on sale at St. Luke's Hospice. St. Luke's rang me to say one of their patients would like to meet me. They pointed out that she, as a rule, had no visitors, relations or what ever. So I felt privileged to be able to visit her. We had a good chat for about an hour. She recalled all her old memories. Just listening to her had confirmed the fact that everybody has a book inside them. She was truly a remarkable old lady. When I questioned her on how the people at St. Luke's were looking after her, she replied, "Wonderful. The only thing I miss is feeding the birds. At home I put food on a bird table and sit for hours looking out at the birds."

On leaving the old lady, I casually mentioned to one of the staff her story about feeding the birds. A week or so later I visited St. Luke's. The old lady I had visited called out, "Fred, Fred." I got to her bedside. She went on to tell me that after my visit they repositioned her bed by a window. She pointed to a bird table outside and said that the nurses took her outside twice a day to feed the birds.

The cost to St. Luke's nil. The personal care, to the old lady, is priceless.

Long live St. Luke's.

One fallacy I must lay to rest is that present day people do not care for others like they used to in days gone by. A couple of years ago B.B.C. Radio Sheffield ran a campaign to raise money for 'Bluebell Wood,' a much needed children's hospice.

They thought it would be a success if they could raise £50,000. Well everyone at B.B.C. Radio Sheffield threw themselves into the campaign. The result was that the total amount raised was £400,000. All of it was raised by listeners from all walks of life in South Yorkshire and North Derbyshire.

Feel Better

Yesterday is history
Tomorrow is a mystery
Today is a gift
That's why it's known as the present